# Presidents in Florida

*How the Presidents Have Shaped Florida
and How Florida Has Influenced the Presidents*

**Date: 2/27/13**

**324.973 CLA
Clark, James C.,
Presidents in Florida : how
the presidents have shaped**

Pi

**PALM BEACH COUNTY
LIBRARY SYSTEM**
3650 Summit Boulevard
West Palm Beach, FL 33406-4198

*To Randall Healy Clark, Kevin Healy Clark, R. J. Clark, Taylor Clark, Elizabeth Mattei, Michael Gannon, Beverly Kees, David and Marion Colburn, Paul and Susan Robell, and Catherine Hinman. And to my colleagues at the University of Central Florida History Department for their friendship and support.*

Copyright © 2012 by James C. Clark

All rights reserved. No part of this book may be reproduced in any form or by any means, electronic or mechanical, including photocopying, recording, or by any information storage and retrieval system, without permission in writing from the publisher.

Inquiries should be addressed to:

Pineapple Press, Inc.
P.O. Box 3889
Sarasota, Florida 34230

www.pineapplepress.com


Library of Congress Cataloging-in-Publication Data

Clark, James C., 1947-
  Presidents in Florida : how the presidents have shaped Florida and how Florida has influenced the presidents / James C. Clark. -- 1st ed.
    p. cm.
  ISBN 978-1-56164-533-6 (pbk. : alk. paper)
  1. Presidents--United States--History. 2. Presidents--United States--Biography. 3. Presidents--United States--Election--History. 4. Presidents--Travel--Florida. 5. Political campaigns--Florida--History. 6. Florida--Politics and government. I. Title.
  E176.1.C586 2012
  324.9759--dc23
                          2012014440


First Edition
10 9 8 7 6 5 4 3 2 1

Design by Jennifer Borresen

Printed in USA

# Contents

# CHAPTER ONE

## No Presidents for Florida
### Plenty of Candidates but No Winner

Florida is the largest state in the Union never to have sent a president to the White House. Virginia and Ohio claim to have produced the most presidents—eight each—but that's because both states claim William Henry Harrison, who was born in Virginia but moved to Ohio. Both New York and Massachusetts had four presidents born within their boundaries, and North Carolina and Texas had two (although neither of the native Texas presidents was named Bush). Even Vermont had two native sons elected to the nation's highest office.

But Florida has failed to produce a single president. In fact, the two words that best describe the state's efforts to place someone in the White House are "short" and "funny." At the 1924 Democratic National Convention, veteran candidate William Jennings Bryan tried to push the candidacy of University of Florida President Albert Murphree but was greeted by rousing boos from the delegates. Bryan had settled in Miami and become friends with Murphree. But the party was far different from the one that had nominated Bryan three times. Bryan and Murphree, champions of Prohibition, were out of place at a convention loaded with people who wanted to repeal Prohibition.

In 1948 Florida Senator Claude Pepper launched a one-day presidential campaign that *The New York Times* labeled the funniest thing at the Democratic convention. Pepper had seen himself as the true heir to the political legacy of President Franklin D. Roosevelt after Roosevelt's death in 1945. He thought President Harry Truman was a poor leader who had abandoned the New Deal and couldn't possibly win the election.

Others agreed, and they searched for an alternative candidate, going through a long list of prospects without finding anyone who wanted to challenge Truman. Pepper declared his candidacy without being asked. The following day, he withdrew from the race, the subject of jokes rather than the recipient of votes. Two years later, he lost his bid for reelection to the Senate.

Claude Kirk is the only person to campaign for both the vice-presidential nomination and the presidential nomination in different years from different political parties. Kirk served a single term as Florida's first Republican governor since Reconstruction but lost his reelection bid to Reubin Askew. Kirk hoped to be Richard Nixon's running mate in 1968, but Nixon selected the far less flamboyant Spiro Agnew. After his defeat in 1970, Kirk ran for a series of offices—senator, governor again, education commissioner, vice president, and president. In 1983 he entered the race for the 1984 Democratic presidential nomination, saying, "Once a man has held the power necessary to make change, to alter the course of events, to stir the public imagination . . . he is forever hooked."

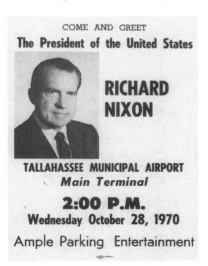

COME AND GREET
**The President of the United States**

**RICHARD NIXON**

TALLAHASSEE MUNICIPAL AIRPORT
*Main Terminal*

**2:00 P.M.**
Wednesday October 28, 1970

Ample Parking  Entertainment

Richard Nixon arrived in Florida to campaign for the reelection of Governor Claude Kirk one week before Election Day. Kirk lost. (Photo courtesy of the State Archives of Florida)

In 1983 the economy was in trouble, and it appeared that President Ronald Reagan might face a tough reelection battle. The economy began to rebound, and Reagan was never seriously threatened, but that didn't stop a record number of Democratic candidates from entering the race, including Kirk and his successor as governor, Askew.

Askew called himself the "different Democrat," but his campaign went nowhere. Many thought he was really running for vice president, and his campaign never gained traction. He did, however, become legendary for bluntness. When NBC correspondent Roger Mudd asked Askew if his campaign was "washed up," Askew retorted, "Not any more than you were, Mister Mudd, when you got passed up for anchor." (Mudd had been passed over several years earlier when Dan Rather became anchor of the CBS Evening News.) The statement was not shown on TV.

Askew's candidacy was doomed before it began. He won a straw poll conducted by Florida Democrats but received only 45 percent of the vote. Former Vice President Walter Mondale trailed with 35 percent, but if Askew couldn't win a majority of the votes in his own state in his own party, how could he win anywhere? In the Iowa caucuses, he finished sixth with just 2.5 percent of the vote, and his campaign was over.

Senator Bob Graham, who, like Kirk and Askew, had been a governor, entered the race for president in 2004. Graham was one of those politicians who had been mentioned as a possible vice-presidential candidate in several elections. It was more of a tribute to the state's electoral vote count than to Graham's popularity. Graham also had a number of drawbacks. He was seen as a competent but bland candidate who was already in his mid-60s and had medical problems. He was easily overshadowed by candidates like Howard Dean and John Kerry. He dropped out on October 3, 2003, the first major candidate to leave the race, and although his name kept popping up as a possible vice-presidential candidate, John Edwards was selected.

Florida has never even had a vice-presidential nominee, and even its representation in the federal Cabinet has been infrequent. Florida was a state for more than a century before it had its first Cabinet member. Alan Boyd of Jacksonville was selected as the first secretary of transportation by President Lyndon Johnson. The most successful Cabinet member was Janet Reno, who was named attorney general by President Bill Clinton. Mel Martinez was named housing secretary by President George W. Bush.

Even though no president or vice president has hailed from Florida, the state plays an increasingly important role in national elections. It now has twenty-nine electoral votes, the same as New York. Only two states, California and Texas, have more.

# CHAPTER TWO

# George Washington
## *The Disloyal Colonies Helped the British*

When George Washington stood on the balcony of Federal Hall in New York on April 30, 1789, to take the oath of office as president, he faced a lengthy list of problems in establishing a new nation. The colonies had hammered together a new Constitution, but there were doubts that it would work. High on his list was the problem with Florida.

Every American elementary school student learns about the thirteen original colonies and their battle for independence from England. But there were actually fifteen original colonies: the thirteen taught in schools, along with East Florida and West Florida. (Some historians believe there were sixteen; they include Canada.) East and West Florida had belonged to Spain until 1763, when control passed to England. As relations between the thirteen colonies and England deteriorated,

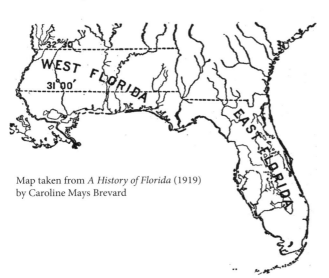

Map taken from *A History of Florida* (1919) by Caroline Mays Brevard

relations between England and the two Florida colonies improved.

One of the things the residents of the thirteen colonies despised was the Quartering Act, which required colonists to allow British soldiers into their homes and to provide them with food and even a ration of liquor. But to the Florida colonists, living on the frontier with marauding Indians nearby, the British soldiers were a welcome sight. Additionally, the British tax on newspapers was hardly a concern in a colony without newspapers. Florida emerged as a champion of British rule, becoming a haven for British loyalists forced to flee the thirteen colonies. In addition to the loyalists fleeing to Florida, scores of slaves seized an opportunity to find freedom in Florida. Finally, the British used St. Augustine as a prison for captured rebel leaders. East Florida colonial Governor Patrick Tonyn wrote to Lord George Germain, the British secretary of state, "There are a number of fugitives from the Neighbouring Provinces, many of whom without a little assistance, have not where withal to support themselves; there are a number of Runaway Negroes from Georgia, who I relieved the Captain of the Navy of, to whom they fled for protection, and twenty-eight Prisoners taken by Lord Dunmore and sent here to be kept in custody. I have committed them to the Fort until these unhappy differences terminate." The rebels launched raids into Florida to try to reclaim slaves and seize British supplies, while the British staged counterattacks into Georgia.

The British surrender at Yorktown in 1781 led to two years of peace negotiations. When the treaty was finally signed, England returned East and West Florida to the Spanish. But the Spain that went back to Florida in 1783 was far different from the Spain of 280 years earlier. The Spain of 1500 was the wealthiest and strongest nation in the world. Its empire covered much of the western hemisphere, its ships moving from the Americas to Spain, laden with gold and silver. When the Spanish first arrived in the early 1500s, La Florida stretched from the Florida Keys to present-day Virginia and west to the Mississippi River. Combined with its Mexican claims, Spain had a North American empire that stretched from the Atlantic Ocean to the Pacific. By 1783 Spain had slipped to a second-rate power and was beginning to lose control of much of its territory.

Florida had never been a moneymaker for Spain, a poor relation to its mineral-rich neighbors. The Spanish clung to Florida to keep other nations out, to spread the Catholic religion, and to protect the treasure ships sailing along the Florida coast on their way back to Spain. Spain had no plans to settle Florida after the American Revolution. The Spanish were spending $30,000 a month (about $650,000 in today's dollars) to support their troops, with no hope of making that much money from the colony.

Spain might not have had that much interest in Florida, but nearly everyone else did. Florida had lost much of its original size to the British colonies, but it still stretched to the Mississippi, including large parts of what are now Louisiana, Alabama, Mississippi, and Georgia. The United States disputed the border and wanted a significant part of those lands to give the future Alabama and Mississippi access to the Gulf of Mexico.

There also were problems with Florida's native tribes, primarily the Seminoles, who set up shop along the northern Florida border and struck into the United States, committing crimes and then moving back into the safety of Florida. With Spain back, the problem of runaway slaves returned. Slaves in Georgia knew that freedom was just a short distance away. At the same time, slave catchers from Georgia and South Carolina were launching raids into Florida to capture runaways. They sometimes caught free blacks in the process. Additionally, freebooters attempted to overthrow the Spanish.

President Washington had his hands full with the Florida problem: Both Spain and the United States claimed parts of present-day Alabama and Mississippi; Spain had forts in the disputed areas; and native tribes in those areas depended upon Spanish control to continue their raids in the United States. Washington selected Thomas Pinckney of South Carolina to negotiate with Spain, but Washington's second term was nearly over before Spain agreed to compromise on the Florida border and to stop inciting Florida Indians to attack plantations in the American. Even after Spain agreed to American demands, problems remained and the situation deteriorated, along with Spain's power.

# CHAPTER THREE

## *Thomas Jefferson*
### *Jefferson Plots to Acquire the Floridas*

Thomas Jefferson was not yet president when he first became involved with Florida, and although he never actually claimed the prize he sought, he set the United States on a course that eventually made Florida part of the nation.

Jefferson was serving as George Washington's secretary of state when he first began talking about the need to acquire the territory controlled by France and Spain that bordered the United States. In many ways, the young nation was at the mercy of European wars. Jefferson knew that a war between England and Spain could send British troops to Spanish New Orleans and restrict American use of the port. He also knew that such a war might end up with Britain regaining Florida, leaving the fledgling United States sandwiched between British possessions. He warned that Britain would "completely encircle us with her colonies and fleets."

"I am…deeply impressed with the magnitude of the dangers which will attend our government if Louisiana and Florida be added to the British Empire," Jefferson told Washington. He urged that if such a war should take place, the United States should become involved. His solution was to seek control of New Orleans and West Florida. "The navigation of the Mississippi, we must have," he wrote.

Jefferson was encouraged when Spain began advertising for Americans to move into Florida. Jefferson saw what the Spanish did not, that the influx of Americans would overwhelm the relatively small Spanish population and make it easier for the United States to take over Florida. He wrote to Washington, "I wish a hundred thousand of our inhabitants would accept the invitation. It would be a means of delivering to us peaceably what might otherwise cost us a war. In the meantime we may complain of this seduction of our inhabitants just enough to make them believe we think it very wise policy for them, and firm them in it. This is my idea of it."

Although some thought a war might be necessary to acquire Florida, Jefferson saw no need for war. He thought Florida would pass "naturally" as the number of American citizens grew.

## A Bid to Buy Florida but No Sale

Thomas Jefferson set out to buy Florida but ended up buying everything except Florida. It began with the treaty with Spain in 1795, when Jefferson was secretary of state. The United States acquired a large part of the Florida Panhandle, which became part of Alabama and Mississippi. The treaty also gave the United States access to the port of New Orleans. Florida, which once reached into the present-day Carolinas and then west to the Mississippi, was once again getting smaller.

Jefferson took office in 1801 and soon faced a new crisis with Spain. In Europe, France's Napoleon had emerged as the greatest threat to other nations. In 1799 he had formed a new government in France, and no one could be sure how far his ambition for more territory would extend. Spain, realizing that its position in North America was becoming weaker, decided to give back control of Louisiana to France. The treaty returning Louisiana to France contained an odd provision: France would own the land, but Spain would govern it. So the United States had to deal with two nations, one aggressive and the other, unable to control its colonies.

In 1802 the Spanish governor in New Orleans announced restrictions on American access to the port, and he declared the 1795 treaty to be invalid. In the United States, the move brought demands for war, although no one was quite sure whom to fight. Some wanted to do battle with France, others with Spain. Alexander Hamilton, who had been

Washington's closest advisor, wrote articles demanding war.

Despite what Americans thought, Napoleon dropped his designs to create a North American empire and became anxious to unload Louisiana. His plans had centered on his crown jewel, Haiti, but everything was working against him. He sent fifteen thousand French soldiers to try to quell an uprising by former slaves in Haiti, but disease and the Haitians nearly wiped his army out. At the same time, he was facing a growing possibility of war with England. During such a conflict, he feared, Louisiana might prove easy for the Americans to take. Napoleon went looking in another direction for empire, toward Egypt.

When James Monroe arrived in Paris on March 2, 1803, as a special ambassador, the timing was perfect. Jefferson had dispatched Monroe with specific instructions: He was to acquire the port of New Orleans and East and West Florida. Congress had appropriated $2 million to buy rights to the Mississippi River, but privately Jefferson told Monroe that he could offer $9,375,000 for the desired land. If Napoleon said no, he was to offer the money for just New Orleans. Napoleon said, "They ask for only one town of Louisiana (New Orleans), but I already consider the colony completely lost." The French quickly offered to sell all of Louisiana for $15 million in cash and debt forgiveness. The agreement, which became known as the Louisiana Purchase, was so massive—the central third of the United States—that the matter of East and West Florida was forgotten for the moment. Jefferson said the treaty "removes from us the greatest source of danger to our peace."

The treaty had come about so fast that it left much to be debated. It took years for the details to be worked out. Left unsaid in the treaty was exactly what the word "Louisiana" meant. The treaty contained no exact geographic points, only the vague statement that the United States was acquiring what France had acquired from Spain. The only clear boundary was the one to the north with Canada. Spain still had large holdings to the west of Louisiana, but it was unclear exactly where. The biggest problem, though, was Florida. Jefferson had acquired a vast amount of land and had purchased New Orleans, but he had failed to win the original prize. West Florida was of strategic importance—controlling the sea approach to New Orleans and including the ports of Mobile and Pensacola, which were vital to navigating inland rivers. Jefferson tried bravely to claim that the purchase included East and West Florida, but there was little to back up his claim, and there was still the presence of the Spanish in Florida. The Spanish had made it clear that Florida and Louisiana were separate entities, administered by different governing bodies, but beginning in 1803, the United States began a twenty-year effort to claim Florida.

The first effort involved simply saying it was so. Jefferson claimed there were solid reasons for believing that the purchase included Texas to the Rio Grande River, much of West Florida, and land as far west as the Rocky Mountains. He offered Spain $2 million for East Florida and the part of Texas he didn't claim, but Spain rejected his offer.

In 1804 he tried another approach—getting Congress to say it was so. Congress passed the Mobile Act, which gave the United States control of the region, including all navigable rivers and streams within the United States that flowed into the Gulf of Mexico. But the Spanish minister to the United States, Marquis de Casa Yrujo, protested, and Jefferson backed down. He was willing to go to war for New Orleans but not for Florida.

In early 1806, Jefferson asked Congress for $2 million for what he called "extraordinary expenses." The money was actually a bribe for Napoleon. In an unprecedented diplomatic move, the United States offered to pay Napoleon to convince Spain to turn over West Florida to the United States. What became known as the Two Million Bill passed Congress despite opposition. Napoleon was willing, but he complained that the money wasn't enough, and the Spanish refused to negotiate. Jefferson's move was condemned by his political opponents and members of his own party alike, one of whom said bluntly, "I consider it a base prostration of the national character to excite one nation by money to bully another nation out of its property."

After leaving the White House, Jefferson continued to push for expansion of the United States. When Florida was finally acquired from Spain, he urged that the treaty be held up and further negotiations be conducted to include Texas in the deal. He even advocated acquiring Cuba.

## The Jefferson Heir Who Moved to Florida

Not only did Thomas Jefferson play a major role in acquiring Florida, but one of his descendants also helped settle the territory. Francis Eppes was Jefferson's grandson. His mother had died when he was only three, and he was raised by his grandfather and aunt, primarily at Monticello, Jefferson's estate. He married and settled on Jefferson's Popular Forest plantation. Jefferson left behind a mountain of debts when he died, and Eppes was the only heir who actually inherited what Jefferson left him.

In 1829 Eppes moved from Virginia to Tallahassee and established a cotton plantation. The territory had been acquired from Spain less than a decade before, and Tallahassee had been the capital for only five years. Like his grandfather, Eppes became interested in politics. He was elected a justice of the peace and then two terms as mayor.

One lesson he had learned from his grandfather was that education was vital. Jefferson had founded the University of Virginia, and Eppes played a similar role. In 1851 the Florida Legislature authorized two seminaries of higher learning. One of the schools was to be on the peninsula, the other in the Panhandle. In 1854 Eppes proposed establishing the Panhandle seminary in Tallahassee, but his plan was turned down. No decision was made at that time, and two years later, he tried again, even offering to contribute $10,000 and a new building.

The legislature accepted the offer, and the Florida Institute in Tallahassee became the State Seminary West of the Suwannee River, with classes beginning in 1857. The seminary later became the Florida Military and Collegiate Institute, then Florida State College, and then Florida Female College. After World War II, to meet the demands of returning veterans, it began admitting men and became Florida State University.

Late in life, Eppes moved to Orlando, where he is buried.

Thomas Jefferson's grandson, Francis Epps, moved to Tallahassee from Virginia.
(Photo courtesy of the State Archives of Florida)

# CHAPTER FOUR

# *James Madison*
## *Encouraging Revolution and Winning West Florida*

Thomas Jefferson tried his best to bluff the entire world. He claimed to anyone willing to listen that West Florida had been part of the Louisiana Purchase. Never mind that maps showed it was owned by the Spanish and not the French.

The northern border of Florida had varied wildly beginning in 1763, when the British acquired Florida from Spain and established the line as the 31$^{st}$ parallel. In 1764 it moved further north about one hundred miles, but when Spain reacquired Florida in 1787, the northern border was not firmly established and disputes began. Those one hundred miles between the 31$^{st}$ and 32$^{nd}$ parallels were significant, because with them came the navigation rights to the Mississippi River. In 1795 George Washington was able to get Spain to agree to the 31$^{st}$ parallel, giving the United States the control it wanted. But while Spain thought the concession would satisfy the Americans, there was no end to the young nation's lust for land. The lesson the Americans learned was that if Spain was pushed enough, she would give up territory.

West Florida was becoming what one historian called the Wild West of the Southeast. Spain had some nine hundred soldiers to patrol the entire region, an impossible task, and it became home to pirates, deserters from the United States Army, criminals, and debtors seeking to escape their bills. Meanwhile, more and more ordinary Americans were moving into the region, demanding responsible government. They had only the militia, populated by settlers from the United States who hoped the Spanish would give up West Florida. William Claiborne, the territorial governor of New

Orleans, reported that the settlers in West Florida were "becoming restless under the Spanish government."

The Kemper Brothers made a number of attempts to seize West Florida between 1804 and 1810. Samuel, Reuben, and Nathan Kemper thought their land would become more valuable if West Florida was acquired by the United States. After the Kempers' failed attempt in 1804 to seize the Spanish fort at Baton Rouge, Secretary of State James Madison quickly labeled it a "criminal attempt" and promised to bring the Kempers to justice. But the Kempers apparently had the secret support of the United States. Governor Claiborne sent an aide, William Wykoff, to West Florida to encourage residents there to foment revolution. Secret meetings were held, and plans for the West Florida revolt were born.

On September 23, 1810, rebels seized the Spanish fort at Baton Rouge, although it wasn't much of a fort, more a ramshackle structure that couldn't hold back any type of uprising. The rebels proclaimed the new Republic of West Florida and displayed its flag: solid blue with a single white star in the center. The republic included parts of what are now Alabama, Mississippi, and Louisiana. St. Francisville (now part of Louisiana) was proclaimed its capital. Fulwar Skipwith, who had helped negotiate the Louisiana Purchase treaty, was named governor. Skipwith, who just happened to be a friend of now President James Madison, made it clear that his republic—its government similar to that of the United States—hoped to become part of the young nation. Meanwhile, Reuben Kemper tried to seize Mobile but was repulsed by the Spanish.

On October 27, 1810, Madison proclaimed the annexation of West Florida. Skipwith wanted to be part of the United States, but he wanted to negotiate terms, not simply be part of a takeover. But Madison sent Governor Claiborne from New Orleans to take control of West Florida, and Claiborne refused to recognize the West Florida government. The Spanish protested but were too weak to do anything about it. They governed what was left of West Florida from Pensacola. Spain held Mobile until 1813, when a military expedition captured it during the War of 1812. The Spanish protested again, to no avail. The acquisition of West Florida had come so easily that it encouraged Americans to consider taking the rest of Florida.

## In Florida, America's First Covert Mission

For the United States, covert operations are nothing new. The nation's first covert operation took place in Florida and was designed to separate Florida from its Spanish owners. It was not the last American covert operation to end in disaster.

In 1811 President Madison sent a secret agent named George Mathews to south Georgia to organize a revolution. Mathews was a strange choice: He was a Revolutionary War veteran with a lifetime of public service, but he was also seventy-two years old. The idea was that once Florida residents set off a "revolt" against Spain, the United States would respond with support. Major Jacint Laval was stationed nearby with two hundred soldiers, waiting to act once the "revolution" was under way.

Mathews called his recruits the Patriots of East Florida and promised them large land grants in Florida—and even public offices—if the revolution was successful. Unfortunately, he found gathering recruits tough going. After a year of trying, he could recruit only nine people, although he also had about seventy members of the George militia. Their target was the giant Spanish fort at St. Augustine. The fort was in miserable condition with a force of just one hundred Spanish soldiers.

Major Laval was supposed to help, but he interpreted his orders differently from what Mathews had in mind. When Mathews asked for ammunition and support from the regular soldiers, Laval told him no, saying, "My orders are to hold and defend East Florida, as you say when offered by the local authorities. These orders don't bind me to use troops to cause a revolution." Florida should be acquired by negotiating with the Spanish, not by military conquest, the major told Mathews.

Mathews insisted that it was President Madison who had authorized the action, but Laval responded, "It is not." Laval ordered Mathews to leave but eventually agreed to let Mathews have forty volunteers. Then the two started arguing again, and the offer of forty men was withdrawn.

Mathews' original goal was to start a revolution against Spain; now he decided to start a revolution against Laval. He had phony charges drawn up against the major, and the charges and countercharges delayed the attack. Eventually, Mathews and his followers took Amelia Island north of Jacksonville and then headed toward St. Augustine. But the Spanish were ready, and Mathews realized he needed substantially more support.

The end was near for the revolution. The United States was drawing closer to war with the British, and Congress had no desire to start a fight with Spain and divert needed men and matériel. Madison couldn't continue the Florida mission, and he also couldn't admit his involvement. He left Mathews twisting in the wind. The revolution dissolved, and Mathews died the following year.

As for Laval, he had had enough of the army in Georgia and requested a transfer. He was moved to the Canadian border, as far away from his Georgia post as possible. He died in 1822, still convinced that Madison had nothing to do with the invasion of Florida.

# CHAPTER FIVE

# *James Monroe*
## *After Two Decades, Monroe Wins His Prize*

James Monroe was the last surviving founding father, a drafter of the Constitution, a secretary of state, a special emissary, and a president of the United States. But the one thing he spent most of his time doing was trying to buy Florida. For nearly two decades, Monroe worked to acquire Florida, starting in the early 1800s, when President Jefferson sent him to France to acquire both East and West Florida and he returned instead with the Louisiana Purchase.

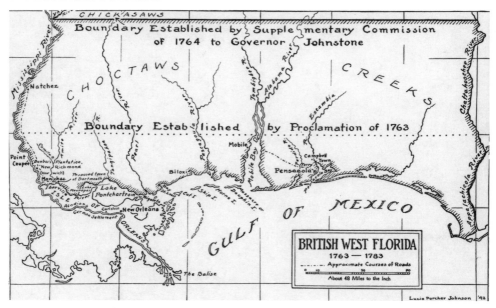

At one time, West Florida stretched to the Mississippi River and north to include much of present-day Louisiana, Alabama, and Mississippi. (Photo courtesy of the State Archives of Florida)

By 1818 West Florida belonged to the United States, but the Spanish still controlled East Florida. Along the Georgia-Florida border, Americans complained that Seminole and Creek Indians were staging raids across the border, attacking plantations, and then fleeing back to Florida. Florida also was becoming a haven for runaway slaves.

Monroe sent General Andrew Jackson, a veteran of problems in Florida, to the border to stop the raids and the escapes. Although he had been sent "to" the border, Jackson was always one to do what he wanted and interpreted his orders rather liberally. He and his men moved into Florida, captured St. Marks, marched on Pensacola, and removed the Spanish governor. He also arrested and executed two British citizens he suspected of aiding the Indian raids.

The reaction from Spain and other nations was swift and critical. Even members of the Monroe administration demanded that something be done. Secretary of War John C. Calhoun recommended that Monroe reprimand Jackson for acting without authority. But one Cabinet member, Secretary of State John Quincy Adams, rushed to his defense.

Adams thought it was the perfect time to try and buy Florida from Spain. Throughout Latin America, Spain was dealing with revolution. In Europe, Spain had fought the Peninsular War—involving France, the United Kingdom, and Portugal—which lasted seven years and left Spain exhausted. Adams saw Florida as just another headache for the Spanish, and it might be better for Spain to strike the best deal possible rather than lose its possession as it had lost West Florida. Adams told Monroe that the United States should open negotiations with Spain.

Adams negotiated with Luis de Onis, the Spanish minister, and a treaty was signed on February 22, 1819. Spain agreed to give up Florida if the United States paid the 1,859 legal claims Americans had against Spain, up to a maximum of $5 million. In exchange, the United States gave up its claim to Texas, and Spain gave up any claims to the Oregon Country. Spain ratified the treaty in 1820; the United States did the same the following year. Although Spain had been able to get the United States to concede that Texas was part of Mexico, Spain was in the process of losing Mexico through revolution.

# CHAPTER SIX

## John Quincy Adams
### *A Presidential Forest Takes Root*

Few presidents have had as much impact on Florida as John Quincy Adams. It's not much of an overstatement to say that without Adams, the history of Florida would have been very different. As secretary of state, he had played a key role in acquiring Florida from Spain, but lesser known is his work in preserving Florida's timberland.

The live oak trees found in Southern coastal areas were vital in ship construction until metal ships were introduced in the late 1800s. The shape of the trees made them perfect for ships' hulls. Unfortunately, the trees were harvested indiscriminately, as there was a virtually endless list of uses for the wood besides shipbuilding. Beginning with the Washington administration, people were concerned about the future of the trees. In 1794 the Navy Department warned that only a forty- to fifty-year supply of the crucial lumber remained. In 1799 Congress passed the Timber Act, which gave President Washington the power to buy timberland to preserve the trees. In 1820 President Monroe reserved lands in Louisiana and even named an official to protect the trees. Of course, it was impossible for a single person to watch a large forest at all times. By 1827 half of the available lumber in the South had been stripped, and the prediction of 1794 appeared to be coming true.

The government sent an agent to Florida to determine how much of the live oak forest remained. The numbers were staggering: As much as two million cubic feet of lumber had been stolen and shipped out of the country. Entire forests had been removed up to fifteen miles inland from the coast.

Adams was passionate about the tree issue. He had even conducted his own research into the preservation of trees. In his diary, he promised to start his own nursery and planted six cork oak trees at the White House: "My passion is for hard, heavy, long-lived wood, to be raised from the nut or seed—requiring a century to come to maturity and then to shelter, shade or bear Columbia's thunder o'r the deep for one or two centuries more." He asked America's overseas consuls to send him literature about trees from tree scholars in other countries. He recorded in his diary that he had received plants from nations as far away as Morocco and Brazil.

Under the Adams administration, the United States government purchased sixty thousand acres near Pensacola. In December 1828, workers began clearing the land and planting young live oaks, but the timing was terrible. Adams lost the November election to his old enemy, Andrew Jackson. Not only did Jackson not like the idea of the government being involved in such activities, he and Adams had become such bitter enemies that anything Adams liked, Jackson hated. Jackson put a stop to the West Florida experiment and went as far as trying to prove that corruption had been involved in purchasing the land. Jackson's administration moved to cancel the project. It died a slow death, killed by politics and long-standing animosities.

## The Dream of a Cross-Florida Canal Begins

The early Spanish explorers in Florida thought there must be a water route across the peninsula. Early maps show large rivers crossing the state—more wishful thinking than fact. When Florida became part of the United States, calls began for the federal government to build a canal across Florida so ships could avoid going around the peninsula. For nearly two centuries, it would remain a dream, at times coming agonizingly close to reality. In all, a dozen presidents took positions on the canal, ranging from strong support to determined opposition.

In 1824, at the end of James Monroe's administration, Congress authorized the army to establish a board to study potential locations for canals. One possibility was a canal "from the river St. Johns across Florida

Neck, to the Gulf of Mexico. . . . Should it prove practicable, its beneficial effects would be great, comprehensible, and durable. The whole of the Atlantic and western states would deeply partake in its advantages."

The election of John Quincy Adams that year seemed to be a boon for the canal supporters. He believed that the federal government should build canals and roads to help the economy of the developing nation. Under his administration, Congress made the first move in 1826, agreeing to spend $20,000 for a preliminary survey. The Army Corps of Engineers organized a group of respected engineers who looked at two routes: The first started on the Florida-Georgia border and went through the Okefenokee Swamp and into the Gulf of Mexico at Apalachicola Bay; the other went from Jacksonville along the St. Johns River to the Gulf.

Both teams encountered problems and delays, so many that General Simon Bernard traveled from Washington to Florida to investigate the issue. He spent two months in Florida and returned to Washington to personally brief the president: "A ship canal across the isthmus of Florida was impracticable and that the most that could be effected was a canal six feet deep for steamboats."

The two teams of engineers sent to Florida returned with positive reports, but Adams listened to Bernard. The report Congress received in the final days of the Adams administration was not what Floridians had been hoping for. It did favor the St. Johns route, if a canal should be built, but effectively eliminated the other route forever.

The first push for a canal had failed.

# CHAPTER SEVEN

# Andrew Jackson
## In the Middle of a Scandal, a Move to Florida

In the early 1830s, Peggy O'Neale was known throughout the nation as the woman in the middle of a major Washington scandal involving her husband, a Cabinet member, and the president of the United States.

Peggy's parents ran a boardinghouse and tavern that played host to many members of Congress. Peggy was educated in New York and gained attention for her intelligence and beauty. When she was eighteen, she married a young navy purser. She also became friends with two visitors to her parents' boardinghouse, Andrew Jackson and his close friend, Senator John Eaton. Her husband was often at sea, and during his absence, Eaton became her regular escort.

Rumors began to circulate about the two, and when her husband died, Peggy married Eaton. Washington was rife with speculation about the couple, and soon Jackson and his Cabinet were taking sides in the growing scandal. During Jackson's first term, there was a division over who should be vice president during his second term. Vice President John C. Calhoun wanted to keep the job, but his wife wanted nothing to do with the new Mrs. Eaton and her husband. Calhoun sought to discredit Eaton in the eyes of Jackson and to influence his decision about a running mate. But Calhoun was wrong. Not only was Eaton one of Jackson's closest personal friends, but the president also saw Eaton as a man who had been the victim of unfair rumors. Jackson's wife, Rachel, had also married young but had separated from her husband, who went to Virginia and claimed to have obtained a divorce. She married Jackson without knowing that her husband had lied. When Jackson ran for president in 1824, political opponents labeled Rachel an adulterer and hounded her. Jackson lost the election, but the attacks continued and increased in 1828, when Jackson ran again. Jackson won that election, but Rachel died shortly afterward, and he blamed her death on the constant attacks. When Eaton and his wife came under attack, Jackson saw a replay of what had happened to him and Rachel.

Jackson defended the Eatons and forced the resignations of Calhoun's supporters in his Cabinet: Navy Secretary John Branch, Treasury Secretary Samuel Ingham, and Attorney General John Berrien. Calhoun was dropped from the ticket for Jackson's second term and saw his dream of eventually reaching the presidency dashed.

In 1834 Jackson rewarded his old friend Eaton by naming him territorial governor of Florida. Perhaps it was a way to get the Eatons away from the gossip and snubs in Washington. In Tallahassee Peggy drew good reviews for her performance as the territory's first lady. She and her two daughters went swimming in the lake behind the governor's mansion. It was an era during which women avoided the sun—a tan usually meant you labored

Peggy Eaton was in the midst of a scandal in Washington when she became Florida's first lady. (Photo courtesy of the State Archives of Florida)

outdoors—and women with social standing seldom went out without umbrellas. But Mrs. Eaton liked the sun, began sunbathing, and developed a tan.

After two years in Tallahassee, Eaton was named ambassador to Spain. Before leaving, he and his wife did something that angered many Floridians. The couple hated slavery, and seven workers in the governor's mansion were slaves. Peggy O'Neale Eaton freed all seven of them.

## Making a Career of Fighting Indians

The Seminole Indians were not among the original Florida tribes. They first arrived in Florida in the early 1700s and became adept at playing sides, taking advantage of the political situation with other tribes and with the United States.

Even before the United States acquired Florida, General Andrew Jackson invaded the Spanish territory to stop the Seminoles from launching attacks into Georgia from Florida. For the Seminoles, it was nothing short of a disaster when the Spanish sold Florida to the United States. In 1823 some Seminole leaders met with government officials

General Andrew Jackson inspects American troops as the Spanish turn Florida over to the United States after the 1821 treaty. (Photo courtesy of the State Archives of Florida)

north of St. Augustine and signed the Treaty of Moultrie Creek. It gave the Seminoles a reservation that included much of the Florida peninsula—about four million acres that no one wanted or could see a use for. At the center of the territory was present-day Orlando.

But problems surfaced almost from the beginning. The Indians didn't like being confined—even if it was to four million acres—and white settlers began moving into what was supposed to be Indian land. What's more, the Seminoles continued to give refuge to escaped slaves. Then in 1829, Andrew Jackson, legendary Indian hater, became president. Jackson convinced Congress to pass the Indian Removal Act, which called for the often forcible relocation of tribes from the east—primarily Georgia and Florida—to Arkansas.

In 1832 the Treaty of Moultrie Creek was declared void by the Florida legislature. Even though the state lacked the authority to invalidate a federal treaty, this bold move showed the mood in Florida. While most of the Georgia Indians headed west in what became known as the Trail of Tears, the Seminoles resisted. Seminoles who agreed to accept money in exchange for moving were often beaten or killed by other Seminoles.

Seven Seminole chiefs met with government officials at Payne's Landing in 1832 and agreed to head west to inspect the lands the government had offered for resettlement. When they returned in 1833, they signed a treaty, but immediately questions and problems arose. First, there were more than thirty Seminole chiefs in Florida, so the seven represented only a small portion of the tribe. Also, had the seven acted under duress or taken bribes?

Still, the government ordered all Seminoles removed from Florida by January 1, 1836. Jackson bluntly told the Indians that if they didn't move, "I have then directed the Commanding officer to remove you by force." But instead of packing their bags, the Indians prepared for what became known as the Second Seminole War. While the army increased its military presence in December 1835, the Seminoles attacked an army supply column. The Indians, in turn, were attacked by militiamen. The Indians began playing hide-and-seek, appearing suddenly to fight and then disappearing into the swamps and forests. Just before Christmas, about one hundred soldiers left present-day Tampa and walked into an ambush on December 28 that killed almost every man. The Seminoles also attacked a fort in present-day Ocala. The army suffered significant losses and retreated.

The Seminoles thought they had won the war, but the Americans were not about to give up. Gradually, the might of the United States overwhelmed the Indians. By 1842 nearly four thousand Seminoles had agreed to accept cash payments and had been transported to the West. About five hundred Seminoles remained, but they retreated into the Everglades, out of reach of the government. The Americans might have thought the Indian wars in Florida were over, but a third war with the Seminoles loomed.

The Battle of Palaklaklaha is depicted in this engraving from the Second Seminole War. (Photo courtesy of the State Archives of Florida)

# CHAPTER EIGHT

## Martin Van Buren
### For the Indians, Van Buren Is No Improvement

Andrew Jackson spent decades fighting, killing, and moving Indians. The various Indian tribes might have hoped that his chosen successor, Martin Van Buren, would be different. Noted for his diplomacy, Van Buren avoided strong partisan statements, but Jackson's former vice president proved to be just as hostile to the Indians as Jackson had been.

In the fall of 1838, Van Buren ordered the removal of 18,000 Georgia Cherokees to present-day Oklahoma. More than 4,000 Indians died during the 116-day forced march. Additionally, Seminole Chief Osceola was captured by a trick that infuriated even many white Americans. General Thomas Jesup set up what were supposed to be peace negotiations with Osceola, but when the chief arrived under a flag of truce, he was captured and imprisoned in St. Augustine. Jesup and Van Buren were condemned for what were seen as actions beneath the dignity of a great nation.

Osceola was moved from St. Augustine to Fort Moultrie in South Carolina. Many white people visited Osceola there, and he became a popular figure. The chief died of malaria just three months after his capture, however, and was buried with military honors at Fort Moultrie.

Like a number of his successors, including Abraham Lincoln, Lyndon Johnson, Richard Nixon, and George W. Bush, Van Buren experienced war weariness. Popular support for the war was waning. Van Buren had increased the size of the army, and in what was then a very small federal government, the war was a major cost. Additionally, the problem of rooting out the Indians seemed endless. The Seminoles could escape into the Everglades and never be found.

Van Buren sent Commanding General of the Army Alexander Macomb to negotiate a treaty with the Seminoles. After the incident with Osceola and the previous broken treaties, the Indians were distrustful. Finally, in 1839, Macomb made yet another agreement with the Indians— peace in exchange for land in south Florida. At first the treaty seemed to hold, but within ten weeks, Indians attacked a trading post, and the Second Seminole War resumed. The army searched for the Indians, resorting to a novel method to track them down: using bloodhounds from Cuba. However, there was a national uproar at the thought of the animals attacking the Seminoles, including women and children. In response, the secretary of war ordered that the dogs be kept muzzled and leashed. The entire controversy was for nothing, however. The dogs proved useless in swampy Florida, and the idea was soon abandoned.

Van Buren's single term in office was plagued by the Second Seminole War and the collapsing economy. Strangely, the two were related. The Indians were being moved to make way for land speculators, but the resulting rampant land speculation brought about the collapse of the economy. When Van Buren ran again, he lost overwhelmingly in the Electoral College. Florida was not yet a state, and residents couldn't vote.

# CHAPTER NINE

# John Tyler
## Tyler Proves a Friend to Statehood

It took twenty-four years for Florida to become a state, and the process proved to be a complicated one. First of all, did Floridians even want statehood? Statehood might seem like a natural goal, but in a number of territories many residents didn't want it. Becoming a state meant taking on significant financial obligations. Residents used to having the federal government pay most of the costs of road-building and administration would have to pay these bills themselves. In a developing area, the costs could be high, and if the population was small, each resident's share would be that much larger. Most officials in a territory were named by the president. Statehood allowed residents to select their own officials, but that too carried a high cost. Secondly, would Florida be one state or two? Since the days of Spanish rule, Florida had been divided into East and West Florida, and Floridians wanted to enter the Union that way.

In 1838 fifty-six men met in St. Joseph, a growing town in the Panhandle, to take the first step toward statehood: drawing up a constitution. The delegates sent the constitution to Washington in early 1839, but final approval took six years.

In the 1840 census, Florida reached a population of 55,000, close to the 60,000 minimum required to become a state, although half of the population were slaves ineligible to vote. Slaves were a major impediment to statehood. The problem was the growing national fight over slavery. Slave states and free states each held the same number of votes in the United States Senate, which meant that no legislation could pass unless the two groups agreed. In the House of Representatives, the North was rapidly gaining seats because of its increasing population, and the president could come from either the North or South. In the Senate, the South could make a stand.

Florida would come into the Union as a slave state, tipping the balance to the South. An agreement had been reached to admit states in pairs, free and slave, to keep the balance. But if Florida entered as two states, it needed two matching free states. Furthermore, leaders in the North were reluctant to admit two new slave states.

Florida would be paired with Iowa, a free state. But Iowans were more reluctant than Floridians to seek statehood. In 1840 they voted against statehood by a three-to-one margin. Two years later, they said no again. Finally, in 1844, the voters said yes, but they imagined a much larger state for themselves, one stretching into present-day Minnesota and including Minneapolis. When Congress said no to those boundaries, the Iowa voters rejected statehood once again. Florida had been waiting for five years, and Iowa still could not agree on statehood.

Florida had a friend in President John Tyler, a pro-slavery Southerner. Tyler became president upon the death of William Henry Harrison in 1841. He was the first vice president to become president, and no one was sure exactly what that meant. Did Tyler actually become president, or was he an acting president? Should another election be held? Tyler knew what he wanted: to be president. He ignored those who called him "His Accidency" and returned mail addressed to "Acting President John Tyler." Tyler may have been president of the United States, but his true loyalty was to Virginia. That became clear in 1861 when Tyler abandoned the Union to become a Confederate congressman.

Tyler wasn't about to wait on Iowa. On his last full day as president, he signed the legislation to admit Florida as a state, which became official on March 3, 1845. Iowa didn't become a state until the end of 1846, nearly two years later. Congress had planned to pair Florida and Iowa, but the delay was so long that Texas was admitted to the Union between them.

# CHAPTER TEN

# Zachary Taylor
## The President Who Knew Florida

The election of 1848 was the first in which Floridians could cast presidential ballots. Zachary Taylor, the Whig candidate, was almost a favorite son, having spent several years in Florida fighting Indians. The last Whig to win the presidency, Taylor defeated Democrat Lewis Cass in a close election. Florida had just three electoral votes—the minimum for a state—which Taylor won by beating Cass in the popular vote: 4,120 votes to 3,083. In the national vote, Taylor defeated Cass with just 47 percent of the total vote.

## Building National Fame Fighting Indians

By 1837 the United States Army was running out of major generals. There were only four in the entire army, and two of them, Edmund Gaines and Winfield Scott, had already tried to suppress the Seminole Indians and failed. Finally, Major General Thomas Jesup was called in early 1837 to lead the army in the Second Seminole War. Jesup changed tactics, dramatically increasing the number of soldiers under his command to nine thousand and seeking to wear the Indians down.

There were signs that his strategy was working: Several chiefs surrendered and others were captured. Jesup organized his army for a sweep down the peninsula, pushing the Seminoles to the south. There would be three columns, including one led by Colonel Zachary Taylor, starting at Fort Brooke—the site of present-day Tampa—and moving through the middle of the state. Taylor's column was the first to see fighting as his one thousand men headed toward Lake Okeechobee in south Florida.

On Christmas Day, he caught the Indians on the north shore of the huge lake. The Indians were ready to fight, even though they were outnumbered two to one. Taylor sent in two hundred soldiers to attack the four hundred Indians, but they were soon driven back. He sent in another infantry group of two hundred soldiers, but after suffering heavy causalities, they also withdrew. A final assault by 160 soldiers succeeded and drove the Indians back toward the lake. The Indians were able to escape, however, and only about a dozen were killed. Taylor suffered many times that number of deaths, yet the army was desperate for any victory, and word went out that Taylor was a hero.

Jesup attempted to negotiate a treaty with the Indians, but his superiors in Washington rejected his proposal to leave the Seminoles alone to live south of the lake. Jesup asked to be relieved of command, and Taylor took his place. The nation was growing tired of the war, and the costs of fighting kept mounting. Taylor's strategy was to construct small forts in north Florida to keep the Seminoles in south Florida. Settlers who were moving into Florida had no desire to claim land in south Florida, so there was no conflict.

It appeared briefly as though the war might be over, but an Indian attack reignited the fighting. Taylor dramatically reduced the violence,

General Zachary Taylor rose to national fame as the commander of troops fighting against the Seminole Indians. (Photo courtesy of the State Archives of Florida)

but he could not eliminate it. In 1840 near Gainesville, four soldiers were attacked; one was killed and two were never seen again. Six members of an acting troupe were killed near St. Augustine, and a mail carrier was ambushed near Jacksonville. Taylor must have realized the war could not be won, and after serving longer than any other Florida commander, he asked for a transfer.

Although he had not been able to defeat the Indians and there would be another Seminole war, Taylor had become famous. His command during the Mexican-American War enhanced his hero status and helped propel him into the White House in 1849.

## A Fort Becomes a Presidential Tribute

Zachary Taylor died midway through his term. To honor him, the government named its newest fort after him. Construction on Fort Taylor at the southern tip of Key West had begun in 1845 and wasn't completed until 1866. Union soldiers seized the unfinished fort and held it throughout the Civil War. Captured Confederate ships were docked at Fort Taylor, and by the end of the war, there were 299 Confederate ships there. Fort Taylor also played a role in the Spanish-American War, during which the fort became a key post for ships and soldiers bound for Cuba. Originally, the fort was surrounded by water, and a walkway linked it to the mainland, but shifting silt has left the fort landlocked.

Construction on Fort Taylor in Key West was only partially complete when it was named for him. (Photo courtesy of the State Archives of Florida)

# CHAPTER ELEVEN

# *Franklin Pierce*
## *New President, New War*

The Whig party tried to keep the presidency in 1852 by nominating war hero Winfield Scott. Democrat Franklin Pierce won easily, taking 254 electoral votes to Scott's 42. Florida and the rest of Deep South went for Pierce. The vote in Florida was 4,318 for Pierce and 2,875 for Scott.

## The Third and Final Seminole War

President Pierce may have thought the problems with the Seminole Indians in Florida were over. The Second Seminole War had ended in 1842, and most of the Seminoles who were not forced to move west had fled into the Everglades to avoid American troops. Then, in 1855, an army survey party working in southwest Florida was attacked by Seminoles. The Indians claimed that the survey party had wantonly destroyed the vegetable garden of the last remaining Seminole chief in Florida, Billy Bowlegs. The following June, Indians attacked a homestead, and a bloody two-day battle erupted. The skirmishes continued into 1858. The army captured a number of Seminoles and forced them to move west.

Although it is called the Third Seminole War, this conflict lacked the violence of the first two. It was a war of attrition, and by the time it was over, only a hundred Seminoles were left in the state, and they had been driven deeper into the swamps.

# CHAPTER TWELVE

# *James Buchanan*
## *Dealing for a Fort*

By 1856 the Whig party was dead, and the Republican Party was born. The Republicans nominated John C. Fremont, and the Democrats chose the party's old war horse, James Buchanan. Former President Millard Fillmore, a Whig, refused to join the Republican Party and instead led the American party, which was anti-immigrant and anti-Catholic. Battle lines for the upcoming Civil War were already being drawn: Fremont was a strong candidate in the North, while Buchanan carried the South. Florida voters didn't even have a chance to support the Republican, since his name wasn't on the ballot. In a state controlled by slave-owning Democrats, voters weren't given an opportunity to vote for the party believed to be anti-slavery. Florida voted 6,358 for Buchanan and 4,833 for Fillmore, who had the best showing in history for a third-party candidate, with 20 percent of the vote. Of course, with Fremont off the ballot in the South, Fillmore was the only other choice.

## The President Fails to Act, and War Comes

In every survey, James Buchanan ranks at or near the top of the list of worst presidents. Buchanan's lack of action in the year leading up to the Civil War convinced many that his behavior ranged from incompetence to outright sympathy for the Southern states.

In late January 1861, former Florida Senator Stephen Mallory, who was to become the Confederate navy secretary, sent Buchanan a telegram saying that Confederate forces would not attack Fort Pickens outside Pensacola if Buchanan made no attempt to reinforce it. Within twenty-four hours, Buchanan agreed to the Southern demands, issuing the following order: "Upon receiving satisfactory assurances from Mr. Mallory and Colonel Chase that Fort Pickens will not be attacked, you are instructed not to land the company on board the *Brooklyn* [U. S. Navy ship], unless said fort shall be attacked, or preparations made for its attack. . . ."

What became known as the Fort Pickens Truce was set. Although it was yet another sign of Buchanan's weakness, the deal was the worst one Mallory ever made. The delay in launching an attack allowed the Union forces inside Fort Pickens to build up their defenses, and Mallory quickly realized that the result of his no-attack compromise was that Fort Pickens controlled the entrance to Pensacola Bay. That meant that the excellent ship-building facilities at the Pensacola Navy Yard were lost to the Confederacy.

Florida Governor Madison Perry anticipated secession by Florida and began acquiring federal facilities: the Apalachicola Arsenal and its weapons; Fort Marion, the old Spanish fort in St. Augustine; the St. Francis Barracks, also in St. Augustine; Fort McRee, off Pensacola; and Fort Clinch, north of Jacksonville. As Perry snapped up federal installations, Buchanan took no action.

A deal between Buchanan and the new Confederates left Fort Pickens in Union control throughout the war. (Photo courtesy of the State Archives of Florida)

## CHAPTER THIRTEEN

# Abraham Lincoln
## Florida in the Civil War

In 1860 war clouds were already gathering. The Democratic Party had fallen apart at its convention, and a series of candidates had emerged. John C. Breckenridge, vice president under James Buchanan, represented Southern Democrats. John Bell represented the remains of the defunct Whig party, and Stephen Douglas was the candidate of mainline Democrats. The Republicans nominated Abraham Lincoln. As in 1856, state officials didn't even put the Republican Party's candidate on the ballot, leaving Florida voters to choose among three Democrats. Breckenridge carried the state easily, with 8,277 votes to Bell's 4,801. Douglas received just 223 votes.

### Lincoln Wins, and Florida Leaves the Union

After Lincoln's victory, cries for secession rose throughout the South. Florida moved quickly, voting overwhelmingly to join the Confederacy in early January 1861. Even though Florida was out of the Union, the federal government had a greater presence there than in any other Southern state. Federal troops held on to forts in Key West and Pensacola, while the Confederates moved quickly to seize Fort Clinch and Fort Marion.

As Lincoln took the oath of office, he began receiving advice from his military advisors about conditions at Fort Sumter in Charleston Harbor and Fort Pickens in Pensacola. Lincoln considered abandoning Fort Sumter and reinforcing Fort Pickens. There was an uneasy truce at both forts: As long as there was no effort to resupply the forts, the South would not attack.

In Pensacola, Confederate forces began to gather under General Braxton Bragg. Even before Lincoln's inauguration, more than a thousand men were waiting to attack the fort. The Confederate ranks kept increasing, until by early April there were more than five thousand men waiting for what everyone thought would be the first battle of the Civil War.

But there were problems carrying out orders at Fort Pickens, and Union efforts to supply the fort with more men and matériel weren't realized until April 11, 1861. Meanwhile, Lincoln had a change of heart and decided to resupply Fort Sumter. On April 12, the Confederates opened fire in Charleston, touching off the Civil War. Two days later, fighting erupted at Pensacola, and the Union navy beat back the Confederates. Skirmishes continued for nearly a year without either side being able to claim victory. Finally, in early 1862, the Confederates abandoned the town, and soldiers were sent to battle sites where they were needed more. Fort Pickens remained in Union control throughout the war.

The Union established a blockade to stop supplies from coming into the South and cotton from being shipped to England. The blockade included Florida, but it was impossible to patrol the state's 3,456 miles of coastline. Goods could be smuggled into Florida, but most of the state's residents were too poor to afford them. They were usually transported to more affluent cities.

Although this drawing shows the Union forces fighting heroically, the Union forces were routed by the Confederates. (Photo courtesy of the State Archives of Florida)

## Fighting for Reelection, Lincoln Turns to Florida

Only one major battle was fought in Florida during the Civil War, a battle fought more for political reasons than military ones. It came about because two men were playing presidential politics in Florida. In early 1864, Lincoln was worried about his chances for reelection in November. There was even talk that his own party might deny him renomination. To win reelection, Lincoln thought he needed every electoral vote he could get. He had won the 1860 election with just 40 percent of the popular vote, and an incumbent hadn't won reelection since 1832.

The challenge would come from Lincoln's own treasury secretary, Salmon P. Chase. While Lincoln was interested in Florida's three electoral votes, Chase was interested in securing Republican convention delegates who might give him the nomination. Chase used what became known as the Direct Tax Law of 1862 to try to take control of Florida. It enabled him to name three tax commissioners in areas occupied by the Union army. Chase sent in three men loyal to him. One of them went so far as to set up a newspaper in Fernandina and fill it with articles about Chase.

The North was tiring of the long war, and although the Union army had posted significant victories, there was a sense that the war might never end. Chase thought a military operation was necessary to eliminate Confederate forces. That's where the story gets confusing. Both Chase and Lincoln needed Major General Quincy Gillmore, who was in South Carolina, to drive out the Confederates.

On January 13, 1864, Lincoln wrote to Gillmore at Hilton Head Island to say that he was sending his private secretary, John Hay, with instructions for him. Strangely, Lincoln didn't inform his own war department of the letter. Hay later claimed the invasion of Florida had been Gillmore's idea. Chase also approached Gillmore, although it is unclear exactly whom Gillmore was really trying to help. Gillmore reported to his surprised superiors that he was sending troops to Florida, primarily African-Americans, "in accordance with instructions which I have received from the President."

Lincoln said he was not worried about Chase, but he was watching

Chase's activities. Union troops held Key West and St. Augustine; Jacksonville passed from Confederate to Union control four times; and the fort in Pensacola was still in Union hands. The invasion began in South Carolina, on Union-held Hilton Head Island. Union troops sailed for Jacksonville, where they drove away a small Confederate force and occupied the city. The orders from Washington were for General Truman Seymour to hold the town, but he disregarded his orders and marched inland with his force of fifty-five hundred men. He wanted to take Lake City. With just 650 residents, it was still the tenth largest city in Florida.

The Confederates brought troops from Georgia and South Carolina—along with Florida soldiers and an influx of volunteers—and gathered at Olustee, a village about a dozen miles from Lake City. The Confederates had about five thousand men, slightly fewer than the Union forces. Confederate leaders proved to be better than their Union counterparts. Union soldiers were thrown on the defensive, and soon the rout was on. The Union army sustained a 40-percent casualty rate, the highest of the Civil War.

The remaining Union troops withdrew to Jacksonville, ending Lincoln's plan to bring Florida back into the Union. Since Florida was a part of the Confederacy, the state's residents didn't participate in the 1864 election. Fortunately for Lincoln, he didn't need Florida's three electoral votes anyway, easily defeating his opponent, former general George McClellan.

There were more military skirmishes, but Florida remained in the Confederacy for the rest of the war, although by the end the Union held major parts of the state. Tallahassee was the only Confederate capital east of the Mississippi not captured by the Union army.

## Florida Farm Boy Plots to Kill Lincoln

Florida had the smallest population in the Confederacy, but it still sent 15,000 young men marching off to war, the highest percentage per capita in the South. Lewis Powell and his two brothers, the sons of a Baptist minister from Live Oak, joined the Second Florida Infantry as soon as the war began.

In 1863 Powell was captured at Gettysburg but escaped and joined Mosby's Rangers. Powell then deserted and crossed Union lines to surrender. He swore allegiance to the Union, changed his name to Lewis Payne, and settled in Baltimore. He apparently met John Wilkes Booth when Booth was performing in a play in Richmond. In 1865 the two reconnected, and Booth told Powell of his plan to kidnap Abraham Lincoln and demand independence for the Confederacy in exchange for the return of the president.

The kidnapping plot ran into difficulties, and when General Robert E. Lee surrendered his Confederate army, the kidnapping plot became an assassination plot. Booth would assassinate Lincoln; Powell would assassinate Secretary of State William Seward; and another conspirator would assassinate Vice President Andrew Johnson.

Lewis Powell, a Confederate soldier from Live Oak, Florida, was executed for his involvement in the conspiracy to kill Lincoln, Vice President Andrew Johnson, and Secretary of State William Seward. (Photo courtesy of the State Archives of Florida)

Powell seemed to have the easiest job: Seward had been seriously injured in a terrible carriage accident and was confined to his bed. On the night of April 14, 1865, Powell knocked on the door to Seward's home and told the servant he was bringing medicine for Seward but had to deliver it personally. The heavyset Powell, who stood over six feet tall, pushed the servant aside and rushed up the stairs. He encountered Seward's son Frederick and tried to shoot him, but the gun misfired.

Powell reached Seward's bed and began stabbing him, slashing his neck, but even in his weakened condition, Seward managed to roll off the bed and escape Powell. Another Seward son, Augustus, entered the room and grabbed Powell, but Powell shook loose and ran down the stairs.

Powell was supposed to meet Booth but in the confusion couldn't find him. Instead, Powell hid in the woods for three days before returning, disguised as a handyman, to the Washington boardinghouse where the conspirators had gathered. The boardinghouse was the worst place to go, since federal officials had already occupied the house. They greeted Powell at the door and took him into custody. For his role in the plot, he was hanged with other conspirators on July 7, 1865.

In Live Oak, Powell's father heard of his son's arrest and left for Washington. But Lewis had already been executed before he reached the nation's capital. The elder Powell gave up his ministry and farm in Live Oak and moved to the wilderness near present-day Orlando. More than a century later, Powell's descendants moved his body from Washington to a family plot outside of Orlando.

## CHAPTER FOURTEEN

# *Andrew Johnson*
## *The War Ends, but Battles Continue*

Abraham Lincoln's death propelled Andrew Johnson into the presidency. Johnson had been chosen as a unity candidate, a Southern Democrat, on a ticket with a Northern Republican. He was a blank slate as far as what he might do in office. The Republicans, knowing that he had no use for the Confederate leaders, thought he would be tough on the South. Others thought he would carry out Lincoln's fairly lenient policies toward the South after the war.

Although Johnson accepted the end of slavery, he showed no inclination to help the newly freed slaves. This set off a battle with the group known as the Radical Republicans, who wanted to help former slaves and punish the South.

Johnson had six months to carry out his Reconstruction policy before Congress met again. Six weeks after becoming president, he offered amnesty to most former Confederates willing to pledge their loyalty to the United States. High-ranking Confederate officials and those with property valued at more than $20,000 could apply for amnesty.

On July 13, 1865, Johnson offered Florida a simple and largely painless path back into the Union. The state had to adopt a new constitution and ratify the thirteenth amendment, eliminating slavery. Most Floridians welcomed the offer, but some, especially new arrivals from the North, thought it was too lenient. One critic was Treasury Secretary Salmon P. Chase, who asked, "Should Reconstruction be left at the hands of prejudiced Southern men?"

Chase, who thought the South should be punished for its actions, had visited Florida in May. He told Key West Unionists that he and

Johnson were in agreement, although he could not have believed that. Chase, who had considered a run against Lincoln in 1864, was trying to build a political machine for another try for president in 1868.

Johnson had hoped to appoint a native Floridian as provisional governor but ended up appointing William Marvin, a native New Yorker who had come to Key West in 1836 as an appointee of Andrew Jackson. Some thought Marvin had been more sympathetic to the South than to the North during the war. The fact that a number of former slaveholders petitioned for his appointment and even went to Washington to press their case was an indication of Marvin's views. One of the most amazing recommendations for Marvin came from Confederate Navy Secretary Stephen Mallory, who was being held in the prison at Fort Pulaski for his role in the Confederacy.

As for meeting Johnson's requirement for readmission to the Union, the delegates to Florida's 1866 Constitutional Convention did as little as they could. They did support the end of slavery, but that was little help to former slaves. Only whites could vote, hold political office, or serve as jurors. Former slaves who had no means of support could be sold for up to a year after gaining their freedom. African-Americans could not testify against whites in court, and, as during slavery, an African-American counted as only three-fifths of a person.

The convention also called for a pardon for former Confederate President Jefferson Davis and other ranking officials. Governor Marvin cheered the actions. The delegates did everything Johnson asked, following his instructions to the letter, if not the spirit.

Marvin served seven months as provisional governor before being elected to the Senate. David Walker succeeded him in late 1865. He said, "We did all the U.S., acting through its President, asked of us, but do not have our rights." Rejected by the federal government, the Florida constitution never went into effect. Republicans in Congress refused to seat the pro-Confederate officials elected in the South, including former Governor Marvin.

Florida was burning through governors at an amazing rate—four in just nine months. Governor John Milton had killed himself on April

1, 1865; Abraham Allison was removed on May 19, 1865; Marvin served seven months; and Walker took over at the end of the year.

In 1866 Johnson lost control of Reconstruction, and the Radical Republicans in Congress took control, dividing the South into five military districts with the army in charge. Florida was placed with Georgia and Alabama. Finally, in 1868, after the state finally approved a constitution that met the requirements of the Union, Florida was readmitted.

# CHAPTER FIFTEEN

# Ulysses S. Grant
## The Conqueror's Warm Welcome

Ulysses S. Grant easily won the 1868 election, defeating former New York Governor Horatio Seymour. The Civil War was over, but Florida had not yet been readmitted to the Union and therefore couldn't vote in the election. Because so many white Democrats couldn't vote in 1868 and so many former slaves could, Grant, who had conquered the South, carried four of the Southern states that were readmitted. In 1872 Grant easily won again, capturing 286 electoral votes to 66 for Horace Greeley, the New York newspaper editor. Florida could vote in the 1872 election, but the normal voting patterns had been disrupted by Reconstruction. Grant won Florida with 17,763 votes to Greeley's 15,427. The 1872 election also showed that Florida was growing. The state's electoral vote increased from three to four.

### Looking for a Political Comeback in Florida

On September 20, 1879, Grant sailed into San Francisco after a triumphant twenty-six-month tour around the world. The tour had been covered extensively by newspapers, and publishers were ready to print books about it. Grant may have been thinking about traveling to his home in Galena, Illinois, or perhaps to Chicago, site of the upcoming Republican National Convention. Maybe even Washington was in his thoughts, as he considered a return to the White House. Surely, as a mighty throng greeted him in San Francisco, he was not thinking about Sanford, Florida, but within a few months, Florida became vital to his plans.

Although Grant had been the hero of the Civil War, his two terms

© 1999 HARPWEEK®

Presidential candidate Ulysses S. Grant received extensive media coverage during his trip to Florida. (Photo courtesy of the State Archives of Florida)

as president were marked by corruption, both grand and petty. Everyone seemed to have a hand in the till during Grant's tenure. By 1876 he wanted a third term, but the corruption in his administration destroyed any chance of that. The House of Representatives passed a resolution urging Grant not to break the tradition of a two-term limit by seeking a third term.

He left Washington but missed the White House. But whenever his name came up, the media also brought up stories of his corrupt administration. An extended tour around the world would bring him positive publicity and quell the corruption stories. The Grants sailed for Europe, with England as their first stop. Queen Victoria held a dinner for them, and then it was on to the continent. Major newspapers and magazines accompanied Grant, routinely featuring stories about him prominently in their pages. While Grant met with the crowned heads, his popularity back home soared. Indeed, his shortcomings seeming to disappear during the year he was away.

But when he returned in the fall of 1879, the negative stories returned. The Republican convention was months away, and Grant's friends soon realized he had come back too early. Another trip was needed to once again restore Grant's popularity, but this one needed to be relatively short. A trip to Florida, Cuba, and Mexico would do the job. And while Grant was in Florida, he could do some political work. Although the South was solidly Democratic when it came to voting, Southern states still played an important role in picking the nominee. African-Americans, who had no political power in Florida, could cast votes at the Republican National Convention to determine the nominee.

Grant arrived in Florida, accompanied by reporters, in February 1880. *Harper's Weekly*, the nation's leading publication, sent an artist to record the trip in sketches. Grant first traveled by steamboat up the St. Johns River to Sanford to visit Henry Sanford, a former diplomat from Connecticut whose family was extremely wealthy. Sanford moved to Florida in 1873 to try his hand at growing and experimenting with oranges and founded what became the modern orange industry. While in Sanford, Grant took part in the launch of the South Florida Railroad. The line, originally called the Lake Monroe and Orlando Railroad, took people from

Sanford to the village of Orlando, about twenty-five miles away. Completed in November 1880, the railroad opened up Orlando.

Henry Sanford and the former president undoubtedly talked politics. Grant had come to Florida to garner some positive publicity, but he also hoped to boost his chances among Florida delegates to the upcoming Republican convention. By supporting the Republican Party, Sanford was a man who was a century ahead of his time. He wanted to reform the Republican Party from one that depended on African-American voters to one that appealed to white voters. The Democratic Party in the South refused to allow African-Americans to register, forcing them to register as Republicans. In 1944, however, the Supreme Court ruled that the Democrats had to allow blacks to register, and the Republican Party became increasingly white.

Grant moved on to Key West, where there was a parade for him and Union General Philip Sheridan. From there, he went on to Cuba. The trip brought Grant the positive publicity he sought and also helped his political

Ulysses S. Grant rides in a parade in Key West during a tour of Florida in 1879. (Photo courtesy of the State Archives of Florida)

situation: He picked up the support of the entire Florida delegation. At the convention in Chicago, Grant was the leading candidate, with 304 of the 370 votes needed, but opposition was too strong to overcome. For thirty-six ballots, the delegates stuck by Grant and his rival, James G. Blaine. But neither could win. Finally, on the thirty-seventh ballot, the party turned to a compromise candidate, Rutherford B. Hayes of Ohio. The Florida delegation had remained loyal, but Grant's political career was over.

# CHAPTER SIXTEEN

# Rutherford B. Hayes
## The Case of the Crooked Election

The 1876 election was one of the most disputed in the nation's history. It took months to unravel, and no one will ever know who really won, but Republican Rutherford B. Hayes was declared the winner. Florida was at the center of the controversy and ended up producing two sets of returns, both certainly fraudulent. The officially accepted results gave Hayes 23,849 votes to 22,927 for Democrat Samuel Tilden.

### Fraud and Florida Elect a President

On election night in 1876, Hayes thought he had lost the presidency to Samuel Tilden. After all, Tilden held a lead of 250,000 popular votes and had won 184 electoral votes, one short of the number needed to clinch the election. There were still three states that had not reported their results, but Hayes went to bed early, certain of defeat. He wrote in his diary, "The affair seemed over." But Republican Party operatives were not ready to give up, and the battle for Florida's four electoral votes began.

The day after the election, Senator William Chandler, a member of the Republican National Committee, sent a telegram to party officials in Florida: "The Presidential election depends on the vote of Florida, and the Democrats will try to wrest it from us. Watch it, and hasten returns."

In addition to Florida, votes from South Carolina and Louisiana were in dispute. In Louisiana, Tilden led by 6,300 votes, and Hays led in South Carolina by about 1,000 votes. Tilden seemed to be ahead in Florida but only by ninety-one votes. In all three states, there had been fraud by both the Democrats and the Republicans, and it was impossible to determine who had really won. Chandler left for Florida and urged other Republican officials to meet in Tallahassee. Quickly, the City Hotel filled as officials from both parties and reporters from major newspapers poured into the state.

In an exercise that was repeated in Florida in 2000, both sides claimed victory and began lining up their cases. The early Republicans to come to the state saw the Democrats winning by about 150 votes. That led the party to send in another group of party officials to see things differently. A state board met to certify the results, but the makeup of the board determined the outcome. There were two Republican politicians on the board and one Democrat. Each party was allowed ten representatives, who watched as the county-by-county results were read. The lead swung back and forth, but after seven meetings, the board had eliminated enough Democratic votes to certify Hayes the winner by a committee vote of two to one. The Democrats still didn't give up, finding their own state official to certify that Tilden had carried the state. Eventually, two sets of returns were sent to Washington: One said Hayes won; the other, that Tilden won.

In January a new Florida legislature took office, this one dominated by Democrats. The legislature appointed a new canvassing board, which dutifully proclaimed Tilden the winner. But in Washington, President Grant had decided to reclaim the matter from the states and the Congress, thereby guaranteeing a Republican victory. He appointed a fifteen-member commission to decide the matter. The eight Republicans and seven Democrats certified Hayes the winner by, not surprisingly, an eight-to-seven vote. Hayes assumed the presidency, but throughout his term he was hounded by those who claimed his election was a fraud.

Hayes had many political favors to repay to the men who had rigged the election. F.C. Humphreys, a Republican elector, was named collector of customs at Pensacola. Dennis Eagan, the chairman of the Republican State Committee, was named collector of internal revenue. Outgoing Florida Governor Marcellus Stearns got the job as United States commissioner of Hot Springs, Arkansas. Even J.M. Howell, the deputy clerk of tiny Baker County, was not overlooked. He had helped gather fraudulent returns from his county and was rewarded with the post as collector of customs at Fernandina.

Hayes also took care of the non-Floridians. Ohio Governor Edward Noyes was named minister to France, and former Iowa Congressman John Kasson took a post as minister to Austria-Hungary. Even a former slave who helped with the fraudulent returns got a job as night inspector in the Philadelphia custom house. Former Union General Lew Wallace didn't want a job that required a great deal of work. What he wanted was time to write a book. Hayes named him territorial governor of New Mexico, which gave him time to write *Ben-Hur*.

Congress held hearings about the election, revealing all of the sordid details. One of those called to testify was Samuel McLin, the head of the canvassing board. He testified that he had been promised he would be taken care of if he helped the Republicans and that the Democrats promised that he "would not die poor" if he supported Tilden. McLin's payoff was being named associate justice of the New Mexico Supreme Court, but he never got to New Mexico. To the surprise of everyone, Republican Senator Simon Conover of Florida blocked his nomination. McLin returned to his home near Orlando, but the travels and travails had undermined his health, and he died in 1879.

# CHAPTER SEVENTEEN

# James A. Garfield
## A Ghost Town Honors a President

The Democrats were back in control of Florida in 1880, although the Republicans kept the vote relatively close. In the national voting, James A. Garfield of Ohio won a narrow victory over Winfield Hancock. Hancock won Florida with 27,964 votes to Garfield's 23,654, and a shift of only about ten thousand votes in New York would have given the election to Hancock. Florida was back in the Democratic column for the first time since 1856. Democrats would dominate presidential elections in Florida until 1928.

The administration of James A. Garfield lasted just six months. On July 2, 1881, Garfield was shot by Charles Guiteau, a mentally ill man who was upset over repeated rejections of his attempts to be appointed the U.S. consul in Paris. The wound would not have been fatal had it not been for the doctors' repeated, unsterile examinations of Garfield's back wound, which led to a massive blood infection, to which Garfield finally succumbed after three months. Although Garfield's short term produced nothing that affected Florida, he did leave a legacy in the state. His death came as towns were springing up in Florida. Winter Park and other communities named streets and avenues in honor of the slain president.

A group of freed slaves also sought to honor Garfield by naming a community after him. They settled in Garfield, near the town of Enterprise in what is now Volusia County. Enterprise was a major town at the time, a port for the steamboats that brought goods and tourists up the St. Johns River from Jacksonville. Though it had a post office, a train depot, one church with a cemetery, and two general stores, Garfield was never much of a town. Freezes wiped out the citrus crops in the late 1880s, forcing the residents to leave. They were gone by the time of the 1890 census.

# CHAPTER EIGHTEEN

# Chester A. Arthur
## Authur Becomes the First Tourist

Chester Arthur is largely forgotten by history, but he made a major contribution to Florida by being the First Tourist, that is, the first president to visit Florida while in office.

No one had expected Arthur to become president. He had been selected as vice president only to mollify the powerful and corrupt New York political machine. Even members of his own party questioned both his honesty and his competence. When President James A. Garfield was assassinated in 1881, Arthur succeeded him. Few Americans were expecting much from a political functionary, but Arthur proved to be an honest president, pushing through civil service reform.

But the workload affected his health, and by 1883, he had gained weight, grown tired, and was suffering from the early stages of Bright's disease, a kidney ailment. In March he decided to visit Florida for what would become standard practice for future presidents: combining a vacation and politics under the sun.

After the Civil War, Florida slowly began to attract Northern tourists, primarily the wealthy. The resort capital was Jacksonville, where visitors stayed for weeks—sometimes months—to avoid the harsh winters at home. Physicians recommended that their patients go to Florida for their health, and by the early 1880s, more than one hundred thousand tourists were arriving during the winter months. In addition to the warm weather and promises of better health, the abundance of fish and wildlife was also a draw. It just so happened that Arthur was a dedicated fisherman.

In early April 1883, Arthur left Washington on a government

mail train. He was accompanied by Secretary of the Navy William E. Chandler; his private secretary, F.J. Phillips; his chef; and a messenger. Most importantly for Florida, he took with him reporters for major newspapers to write stories about the wonders of the state. He arrived in Jacksonville on April 6 and was greeted by city leaders, a large crowd, a twenty-one-gun salute, and deafening cheers. The original plan was to spend the night in Jacksonville, but after the rousing reception, Arthur set out for Sanford. Why he scrapped his plans to stay in Jacksonville is a mystery. It might have been because the train had arrived very late, the result of a broken coupler. Or it might have been because smallpox had broken out in the city. Before Arthur arrived, twenty-four people had died.

The president boarded a steamer on the St. Johns River for the trip south. He told the reporters he was surprised that Florida was so beautiful. In Sanford, Arthur was the guest of Henry Sanford, who had hosted Ulysses Grant three years earlier. Arthur stayed for two nights and then moved on to Kissimmee. But the reporters noticed a change in his mood. He became irritable and looked bored. They stopped in Maitland briefly and traveled by buckboard to Winter Park, a few miles away. During the journey, the buckboard hit a rut, and Secretary Chandler and a woman were thrown out, but they weren't injured. Reporters commented on the beauty of Winter Park, but the pleasant scene did nothing to improve Arthur's mood. He boarded the train in Winter Park for a brief trip to Orlando. The original plan called for the president to stop and give a speech, but Arthur didn't want to stop. When an aide tried to change his mind, he said, "I say we shall not stop in Orlando." He did agree to go out onto the platform and bowed to the waiting crowd, offering a broad smile. But when the engineer stopped the train instead of just slowing down, Arthur again became angry. He rushed back inside the car in a foul mood. He remained angry during the trip to Kissimmee, where he boarded the steamer *Okeechobee* and sailed on Lake Tohopekaliga. As historian Joe Richardson has noted, the reporters thought they had reached the end of civilization because the telegraph lines ended in Kissimmee.

Fortunately, Arthur's mood improved remarkably when he went fishing in Reedy Creek, which would become famous a century later as the home of Walt Disney World. He caught five ten-pound bass, and reporters proclaimed him a great fisherman, one labeling him the finest amateur caster in the world. Other members of the party were not as interested in fishing and spent their time shooting alligators.

On April 11, Arthur went back to Sanford, suffering from a painful sunburn but otherwise in good spirits. He had agreed to attend a reception with local leaders, but it was cancelled when local citizens argued over who should make the introductions. He told aides that he would have liked to remain in Sanford, but he set off for St. Augustine. To get there, he had to first return to Jacksonville and then travel south down the coast.

Even though his predecessor had been assassinated, Arthur didn't appear to worry about security as he wandered through the streets of St. Augustine alone. On Sunday evening, his party attended services at the African-American Methodist Church and listened to the choir sing for more than an hour. He went fishing and declined an invitation from Governor William Bloxham to visit Tallahassee. Instead, he boarded the USS *Tallapoosa* for Savannah, Georgia.

Arthur returned from his trip south sporting a tan and claiming he was feeling better, but he already had Bright's disease. Within three years, he was dead, one of the youngest former presidents to die. But his trip proved to be a boon to Florida, attracting massive amounts of publicity and putting the state's varied attractions on view.

# CHAPTER NINETEEN

# Grover Cleveland
## A Presidential Push for Tourists

In 1884 the Democrats nominated Grover Cleveland of New York for president. The Republicans chose James G. Blaine of Maine. But it didn't matter who the nominees were: Florida and the rest of the South would vote for any Democrat against any Republican. Cleveland carried Florida, 31,769 votes to 28,031 for Blaine. African-American voters, who were traditionally Republicans, kept the race close.

Cleveland sought reelection in 1888 and easily won the popular vote. But Benjamin Harrison won in the Electoral College, thanks to carrying New York by fifteen thousand votes. In Florida, the Democrats were becoming stronger, while African-Americans were slowly losing their rights. Cleveland received 39,557 votes to Harrison's 26,529.

In 1892 the Democrats again chose Cleveland as their nominee, even though he had lost in 1888. Cleveland was determined to return to the White House. Harrison had lost popularity, and Cleveland received 277 electoral votes to Harrison's 142. The Populist Party candidate, James Weaver, captured just over one million votes and twenty-two electoral votes in five lightly populated states. In Florida, where officials kept Harrison off the ballot, Cleveland easily defeated Weaver, 30,153 votes to 4,843.

## Cleveland Comes to Promote Florida

When Henry Flagler first arrived in Florida in the 1870s, he was one of the nation's wealthiest men, thanks to his partnership with John D. Rockefeller in the Standard Oil Company. Within a few years, he began to

*Harper's Weekly* gave President Cleveland's visit to Jacksonville extensive coverage. *Harper's* was the nation's leading weekly publication. (Photo courtesy of University of Central Florida Library)

develop the state's tourism industry, starting in St. Augustine and heading south until he reached Key West thirty years later. Most of those who stayed at Flagler's Ponce de Leon Hotel in St. Augustine were wealthy, the kind of people who might invest in the state, or buy land, or urge their other friends to do so. Rockefeller built a home in Ormond Beach near one of Flagler's hotels.

By 1888 state officials realized that tourism could be an economic bonanza. Other states were trying to lure visitors. California had launched a public relations campaign aimed at tourists and winter visitors. Florida would need to compete.

Other states had expositions, and Florida's could feature the state's products, including seafood, vegetables, and fruit. But Florida would need something special to make its version stand out. Jacksonville officials invited President Cleveland and his new first lady, twenty-three-year-old Frances. Married just two years to the president, Frances captivated the nation. It was unclear who was a bigger draw, the president or his wife.

The Clevelands left Washington by special train in February 1888, stopping briefly in Savannah before heading for Jacksonville. *The New York Times* described Cleveland's visit as the "greatest event in the history of Jacksonville." The city was wildly decorated with palm branches, fruit, and flowers. The president and first lady were taken to the luxurious St. James Hotel, the finest in the state in the late 1800s and the first to have electricity. Along the route, nearly ten thousand people shouted their appreciation. The couple attended the exposition accompanied by a number of groups: African-American musicians, the "colored" state militia, and white groups, such as the Knights of Pythias. More than one hundred thousand people turned out for the exposition.

Jacksonville officials received the publicity they had sought. Newspapers throughout the nation published stories about the city and the exposition. Northern readers were reminded of Florida's warm weather. Unfortunately, the positive press didn't last. Four months later, yellow fever swept through the city, killing four thousand people and lasting until October. The exposition was largely forgotten, and Jacksonville became known for its diseases, not its flowers.

Cleveland continued his Florida trip in St. Augustine, where he was personally welcomed by Henry Flagler, and then Palatka, at the time a major port city. The president arrived late and managed to anger the mayor and city council because they weren't introduced to him.

In Titusville the Clevelands boarded a boat on the Indian River for a cruise to the community then known as Rock Ledge (today's Rockledge). Other stops included Sanford, where they attended another exposition, and Winter Park, where they stayed at the Hotel Seminole, and the local newspaper reported, "The table groaned with a most tempting array of the finest luxuries known to the culinary art." According to historian Ray Osborne, Cleveland was a frequent visitor to Florida after he left office and was a guest at both the Harvard Canaveral Club and the Harbor Inn in Cape Canaveral.

Cleveland, under the letter "E" in the word "hotel," and his wife, Frances, visited Rock Ledge—today known as Rockledge—and stayed at the Hotel Indian River. (Photo courtesy of the State Archives of Florida)

# CHAPTER TWENTY

# William McKinley
## Freeing Cuba While Boosting Florida

The 1896 election was one of the most dramatic in American history. William Jennings Bryan, the young congressman from Nebraska, received the Populist and Democratic nominations and offered a radical platform for the nation. The Republicans went with William McKinley, the conservative Ohioan who would carry on as his predecessors had done. McKinley won by a wide margin, but Bryan carried Florida: 32,756 votes to McKinley's 11,128.

In 1900 McKinley ran for reelection, and once again the Democrats nominated Bryan. McKinley repeated his victory nationwide, but in Florida Bryan was still the favorite, receiving 28,273 votes to 7,355 for McKinley. The state's campaign to restrict the rights of African-Americans and to strike them from the voting rolls was well under way. African-Americans had been the prime supporters of Lincoln, although they never posed any serious threat to the Florida Democrats.

### War Fever Comes to Florida

McKinley had a new set of problems to solve. From 1868 to 1878, a running revolution in Cuba forced many Cubans to flee to the United States. They settled primarily in Tampa and Key West, where more than six thousand Cubans created a huge cigar industry and made the towns centers of revolutionary fever. Throughout the 1800s, there was frequent talk in the United States of acquiring Cuba, although nothing came of it. But in 1898, as the possibility of a war with Spain came closer, newspapers throughout most of the country stoked the calls for war. Front-page stories—many of dubious veracity—told of atrocities committed by the Spanish government against Cubans.

Cuban revolutionary José Martí was largely responsible for rekindling the revolutionary fever in the 1890s. He set up his headquarters in New York and established nearly two hundred pro-revolution clubs throughout the country, nearly half of them in Florida. Cigar workers contributed a portion of their wages to finance the clubs and the revolution. The money went to buy arms to send to fighters in Cuba. The gun-running turned into an economic boon for Florida ship owners, including future governor Napoleon Broward.

War fever reached a peak in most of the country when the USS *Maine* exploded in Havana harbor on February 15, 1898, killing 250 sailors. The ship had sailed to Havana from the navy base at Key West, and the survivors were returned to the base. While newspapers in most of the country demanded war, Florida newspapers were much more restrained. The *Florida Times-Union and Citizen* in Jacksonville supported the Cubans but said the United States must let them fight their own war for independence.

The newspapers mirrored the mixed feelings of Floridians about a possible war with Spain. Although Floridians supported independence for Cuba, they worried that a war for Cuban independence might become a war of conquest, with Cuba ending up as a territory or even a state. Floridians saw Cuba as an economic threat: The island's economy was almost a mirror image of Florida's. Both had large centers of cigar production; both produced sugar, vegetables, and fruits; and both had developing tourist industries. As part of the United States, Cuba wouldn't have to worry about tariffs and could undercut Florida prices. There also were military concerns. Cuba was just ninety miles from Florida, and Floridians worried that Spanish ships might shell Florida's coastal cities.

McKinley moved to calm Floridians' fears. The War Department established batteries in the coastal cities of Miami, St. Augustine, Fernandina, St. Augustine, and Jacksonville. Home guard units were assigned to Palm Beach, Miami, Pensacola, Palatka, and other towns.

Economic concerns remained, however. McKinley pushed the Teller Amendment through Congress, which promised that the United States would not make Cuba part of the United States. That satisfied Florida business leaders.

As Florida's worries eased, Floridians began to realize that the state's closeness to Cuba could be an advantage. The military would need to include Florida in any military planning, and that meant men and matériel passing through the state. An agent for the Florida East Coast Railroad offered the War Department the line's 367 miles of track from Jacksonville to Miami and 235 miles of steamship service from Miami to Key West.

But there was competition for the military camps. Savannah, Mobile, and New Orleans put in bids. Key West was an obvious choice, except for one shortcoming: water. Although surrounded by sea, Key West had limited drinking water, and that limited how many soldiers and sailors could be stationed there. Leaders in Tampa began to push for their town, pointing out that Tampa was just 223 miles from Havana, closer than Mobile, Savannah, and New Orleans. The War Department ordered seven regiments to Tampa, and leaders in other Florida cities began to lobby for troops.

President William McKinley (left) stands with Governor William D. Bloxham on the steps of the capitol in Tallahassee. (Photo courtesy of the State Archives of Florida)

Tampa may have wanted the soldiers, but the city was grossly unprepared for the thousands who came. The grand Tampa Bay Hotel could serve as a headquarters for the military leaders and journalists, but there was little room for the soldiers. A single train from New Orleans carried five hundred soldiers and had fifty cars, including one for horses, nine for baggage, and fifteen for wagons. By May there were 23,000 soldiers in the Tampa area, overwhelming the town's resources. Tampa's original population of 25,000 was inundated with 40,000 soldiers, journalists, and camp followers.

The ornate Tampa Bay Hotel as it appeared in 1898. The hotel housed the military leaders in the Spanish-American War. (Photo courtesy of the State Archives of Florida)

In June thousands of soldiers left for Cuba, along with 2,300 horses and mules. Twelve thousand men were left behind, and more were on the way, even though there was little chance of more soldiers going to Cuba. Despite the economic bonanza for businesses, the city was growing tired of the soldiers. Finally, soldiers began to leave, and by August 20, 1898, the last were gone, although massive amounts of equipment and 4,000 horses and mules remained. The departure moved quickly. A year after the first troops arrived, there were just two soldiers left to run the single warehouse still operating.

Camps in Lakeland and Jacksonville were actually better suited to the task than Tampa. Camps in Miami and Fernandina, however, were disasters. Miami had been rejected as a camp, but eventually 7,500 soldiers arrived in the middle of a brutal summer. Many of the soldiers had no sewer service, and typhoid fever broke out. Infected water caused other diseases. One soldier wrote to his family that if he owned hell and Miami, he would sell Miami and live in hell. The camp in Miami lasted just a month before it was closed, and the soldiers were ordered to Jacksonville. Fernandina was even more of a nightmare for the military. There was a good harbor but little else, and the men were gone within a few weeks.

Key West had proven to be a good base for a peacetime Navy, but the demands of war showed how inadequate it was. There simply wasn't enough room on the small island for everything. The arrival of more than four hundred Spanish prisoners from captured ships only added to the already overcrowded conditions. Water had to be brought in from Tampa at two cents a gallon.

The Spanish-American War lasted just 123 days, but it left Florida far better off than before. Tampa had seen an influx of new residents and facilities. Key West had vastly expanded port facilities that would serve it well. And as happens in all wars, many of the soldiers who passed through Florida returned to become permanent residents.

## McKinley Seeks Votes and Relaxation in Florida

In the late 1800s and early 1900s, Thomasville, Georgia, became a popular winter resort for wealthy Northerners. In 1899 President McKinley visited Thomasville with Mark Hanna, his friend and political mentor, who had been a regular visitor to Thomasville, combining vacations with politics. In elections, the South was solidly Democratic. But in presidential campaigns, Southern Republicans could play a decisive role in selecting the party nominee. Hanna had traveled to Thomasville in 1896 to look for support among Southern Republicans for McKinley's presidential bid. McKinley won the nomination and the presidency.

During their 1899 meeting in Thomasville, McKinley and Hanna decided to visit Florida. They headed toward the town of Monticello, outside of Tallahassee, and visited the home of Senator Samuel Pasco, who the following month would lose his reelection bid. The railroad had left a special train at McKinley's disposal, and he moved on to Tallahassee, where decorations had been installed throughout the town. McKinley and Hanna went first to the capitol building, where a large crowd had gathered. A reception was held at the Leon House, the city's leading hotel.

Most Republicans in Florida were African-Americans. Although they could not vote in general elections, they could be Republican delegates to national nominating conventions. Although there was no doubt McKinley would be renominated in 1900, Hanna was a cautious campaign manager. After the reception, McKinley went to Florida A&M University, a school established a decade earlier for African-Americans. Students gathered to see the president, and the school's band performed for him. He stayed only a few hours in Tallahassee and didn't make a single speech. He was asked to visit Tampa but declined and returned to Thomasville.

# CHAPTER TWENTY-ONE

# Theodore Roosevelt
## Fighting for His Country—and the Birds

The assassination of William McKinley in 1901 put Teddy Roosevelt in the White House. Three years later, Roosevelt sought the presidency in his own right and easily defeated Alton Parker, an obscure figure whose political career had been limited to a run for chief justice of the New York Court of Appeals. Parker never had a chance and became the first presidential candidate to lose by more than a million votes. Florida remained loyal to the Democratic Party, however, and Parker claimed the state with 26,449 votes to Roosevelt's 8,314. The 1904 election reflected yet another gain in Florida's population: The state now had five electoral votes.

### Roosevelt Leaves Florida and Returns a Hero

Roosevelt was serving as assistant secretary of the navy as relations with Spain over Cuba began to deteriorate. While President McKinley and others hesitated to go to war with Spain, Roosevelt was the loudest voice calling for a battle. He dismissed McKinley as having "no more backbone than a chocolate éclair." Administration officials were wary of Roosevelt, who found he could no longer get in to see the president. His own party tried to isolate him. But public pressure, along with a massive campaign by the nation's leading newspapers, pushed constantly for conflict with Spain. On April 11, 1898, McKinley asked for a declaration of war.

When McKinley called for 125,000 volunteers, Roosevelt was among the first to step forward. His friends and family opposed the idea. His boss, Navy Secretary John Davis Long, wrote that Roosevelt had "lost his head to this folly" but added, "and yet how absurd this will sound, if by some turn of fortune he should accomplish some great thing and strike a very high mark." McKinley tried twice to talk Roosevelt out of it but finally gave up.

Roosevelt would be part of the effort to recruit war volunteers from the frontier. He once worked on a ranch in Dakota territory and knew how to ride and shoot. He headed for San Antonio, Texas, where the men would

Teddy Roosevelt (far right) stands with his officers in Tampa, waiting to embark for Cuba. (Photo courtesy of the State Archives of Florida)

undergo training. There were about fifty Easterners in the group, most, like Roosevelt, from wealthy families. Reporters quickly dubbed the Western contingent Roosevelt's Rough Riders.

The War Department had set up the army's headquarters in Tampa, and Roosevelt and his men spent four days traveling there by train from San Antonio. Roosevelt wrote that they arrived to find "everything connected with both military and railroad matters was in an almost inextricable tangle. There was no one to meet us or to tell us where we were to camp, or issue us food for the first twenty-four hours."

Roosevelt had to spend his own money to feed the men and to commandeer wagons to unload their goods from the train. After five days, Roosevelt was notified it was time to load the ships for the journey to Cuba, but the number of soldiers was far greater than the ships could possibly carry. A third of the men would have to stay behind, along with the horses. Some of the men began to curse.

On the evening of June 7, Roosevelt and his men learned that the ships would load the following morning, and if they weren't ready, the vessels would sail without them. The men were ordered to meet at the railroad track for a midnight ride to the port. They arrived, but the trains didn't. When trains did arrive, some men boarded, but the trains didn't move.

At 3 A.M., Roosevelt was ordered to march to another railroad track, but no train was waiting there either. At 6 A.M., he and his men stopped some coal cars and, after an argument with the train engineer, forced him to take them to Port Tampa, nine miles away. They arrived at the port covered with coal dust. After searching for nearly an hour, they found an available ship, the *Yucatan*. The ship was not at the dock, and Roosevelt's commander, Leonard Wood, seized a small launch to reach the vessel. Roosevelt learned that the ship he was about to use had actually been assigned to other regiments. He hurried back to the nearby train and ordered his men to march double-time to the launch. Once his men were onboard the *Yucatan*, they saw their first action of the war: preventing the two regiments originally assigned to the *Yucatan* from boarding. Some of the other soldiers were finally allowed to board, and the packed ship sailed several hundred yards into the middle of Tampa Bay, where it sat for a week before finally sailing for Cuba.

Roosevelt returned to the United States a famous man. Leading his Rough Riders up San Juan Hill earned him the vice presidency in 1900 and the presidency the following year when McKinley was assassinated.

Teddy Roosevelt (front right) poses with his troops in Tampa before leaving for Cuba and the ride up San Juan Hill that would make him famous. (Photo courtesy of the State Archives of Florida)

## Fighting a Different War—to Save Birds

While Roosevelt was leaving from Florida's west coast, Paul Kroegel was fighting a different type of war on the state's east coast. Kroegel, a German immigrant, arrived in Sebastian in 1881 and settled on the Indian River Lagoon. From his house, he could see Pelican Island, home to thousands of pelicans and other birds that roosted and nested there.

Kroegel was not the only one admiring the beautiful birds on Pelican Island and elsewhere in Florida. Their feathers, perfect for topping off ladies' hats, were in demand throughout the world. Hunters killed them by the thousands. There were no laws to protect the birds, and Kroegel took it upon himself to row a small boat out to the island and stand guard with his gun.

In 1901 the Florida Audubon Society was successful in getting legislation passed in Florida to protect the birds. The society hired four wardens to guard the birds from hunters, including Kroegel. The work was dangerous: Two wardens were killed by hunters.

The birds needed greater protection than the Florida law could provide. Two men who knew of Kroegel's work were friends of Roosevelt's. They visited him at his New York home and explained the situation. Roosevelt was moved and signed an executive order making Pelican Island the first federal bird reservation. He went on to establish a total of fifty-five bird reservations, ten of them in Florida. Kroegel was hired as the first national wildlife refuge manager, but Congress had not appropriated any money for his pay. Instead, the Audubon Society paid him $1 a month. Beginning with five-acre Pelican Island in 1903, the National Wildlife Refuge system now has more than 550 refuges comprising more than 150 million acres.

Establishing bird sanctuaries wasn't Roosevelt's only effort to preserve Florida's natural beauty. In 1908 he created Ocala National Forest, the oldest national forest east of the Mississippi. Choctawhatchee National Forest in the Florida Panhandle, also created in 1908, was turned over to the military in 1940 as World War II loomed. Today it is home to Eglin Air Force Base.

# CHAPTER TWENTY-TWO

# *William Howard Taft*
## *Looking for Votes in Unfriendly Territory*

In 1908 Teddy Roosevelt made a decision he would regret for the rest of his life: He would not be a candidate for reelection in that year's election. But he was able to deliver the Republican nomination to William Howard Taft, his protégé. The Democrats again nominated their old standby, William Jennings Bryan. Taft won easily, except in the South. All but 23 of Bryan's 162 electoral votes came from the South. In Florida, Bryan received 31,104 votes, compared to 10,654 for Taft. Although Bryan served as secretary of state from 1913 to 1915, he would not be nominated again for president. His relationship with Florida was not over, however. In 1913 he bought a home in Miami, and in 1925 he moved to nearby Coconut Grove. He became a spokesman for the new community of Coral Gables, and his daughter, Ruth Bryan Owen, became the first woman elected to the House of Representatives from Florida.

## Republicans Came Seeking Convention Delegates

For Republican presidents and presidential nominees, the South was something of a quandary. In the general elections between 1880 and 1952, Republicans knew that Democrats would almost always carry the South. No matter how distasteful the Democratic candidate might be to Southern voters, he could still count on states such as Alabama, Mississippi, and Georgia coming through for him.

Although campaigning in what became known as the Solid South might be a lost cause for Republicans seeking the presidency, Southern

Republicans were still important in picking the party's nominee. A Republican might be doomed to get only 10 percent of the presidential vote in Alabama, but Alabama's delegates to the Republican National Convention might offer just the support a candidate needed to win the nomination. African-American voters in the South enjoyed few rights, but they usually made up 5–6 percent of the convention delegates.

In the years immediately after the Civil War, Republican presidential candidates generally ignored the South, doing what was called "waving the bloody shirt" to excite Northern voters and increase turnout. Democrats were portrayed as friends of the Confederacy. But once elected, Republican presidents could no longer ignore the South, and their trips to the region became vacations that included politics and national unity-building.

By 1908 the Civil War generation was dying out, and waving the bloody shirt didn't have the same impact. The Republican Party was beginning to change. President Taft all but abandoned the fight for African-American voting rights, and he even supported literacy tests as a requirement for both whites and blacks to vote. Taft was the first Republican president to see a real chance for political gain in Florida. He lured white voters while trying to hold on to black voters. It was clear to many, however, that white Southerners were the voters Taft most wanted.

Another change occurred slowly over the course of several presidencies. When McKinley traveled to Florida, he spoke to crowds that included whites and blacks and even watched a biracial parade. Taft spoke to segregated groups: a dinner with white businessmen, a speech at a black church, for example. The South had begun its move to the Jim Crow era in the 1890s, segregating nearly every aspect of life. Previous Republican presidents had at least paid lip service to the idea of uniting black and white voters, but Taft's trips to the South seemed to do more dividing more than uniting. As one journalist said, "He did so many things that made him unpopular."

# Taft Came to the Celebration Very Late

Taft was supposed to be in Florida in January 1912 to celebrate one of history's greatest engineering feats: completion of a railroad to Key West. Henry Flagler had already built a railroad connecting Jacksonville to Miami. Then he dreamed what many thought was impossible: extending the railroad to Key West, covering more than one hundred miles, mostly over water. It had originally been branded "Flagler's Folly" and written off as an old man's foolish idea.

Instead, Flagler overcame long odds and three hurricanes to make his dream come true. Work began in 1905 and was completed in 1912. He invited President Taft to ride with him on the inaugural trip from Miami to Key West and take part in the celebration. Taft accepted the invitation but had to cancel because of problems in China. Taft had to send troops to Tientsin to protect Americans as the Chinese Revolution raged.

Taft finally made it to Key West in December 1912. A month earlier, he had lost his reelection bid in a three-way race. Now, as a lame duck, he visited Florida on his way to inspect the Panama Canal construction. Upon his arrival in Key West from Washington, he had lunch and then went to

William Howard Taft (to right of man holding top hat) arrives at the train station in Key West in 1912. (Photo courtesy of the State Archives of Florida)

the Naval Station, where he boarded the battleship *Arkansas* for the trip to Panama. Although he spent only minutes at the Naval Station, he became the first president to visit what became known as the Little White House. The rambling building had been built in 1890 for use as housing for navy officers assigned to the island's naval base. Taft was also the first of six presidents to visit Key West, although it would be more than thirty years before the next presidential visit by Harry Truman.

# CHAPTER TWENTY-THREE

# Woodrow Wilson
## Losing a Primary, Winning an Election

The Republicans were badly fractured in 1912. Teddy Roosevelt never got over his decision to give up the White House to William Howard Taft. During Taft's term, Roosevelt became an opponent of his one-time friend and by 1912 had decided to challenge him for the Republican nomination. Roosevelt was far more popular than Taft, but Taft controlled the Republican Party's political machine. In the South, he had complete control and was able to win the nomination. Roosevelt formed a third party and continued his campaign. Wilson won with just 42 percent of the vote, however. Roosevelt finished second with 27 percent, and Taft was third with 23 percent. In Florida, Wilson won easily with 35,343 votes. The 1910 census had shown an increase in Florida's population, upping the state's electoral votes to six.

Amazingly, neither Taft nor Roosevelt finished second in Florida. That spot went to Eugene Debs, the Socialist candidate, who polled 4,806 votes. Roosevelt received 4,555, and Taft got 4,279. In 1916 Wilson faced a much more difficult election. The Republicans united behind Charles Evans Hughes, and Wilson nearly lost. A shift of just two thousand votes in California would have put Hughes in the White House. Wilson easily won in Florida, with 55,984 votes to Hughes' 14,611. Minor candidates also found support in Florida. Socialist candidate Allan Benson received 5,353 votes, while James Hanly, the Prohibition candidate, got 4,786.

# Florida's First Contested Primary: The Fix Is In

In 1912 the Democrats had plenty of presidential candidates to choose from. The leading candidate was Champ Clark of Missouri, the speaker of the House of Representatives, but also in the race were Governor Woodrow Wilson of New Jersey, Congressman Oscar Underwood of Alabama, and Governor Judson Harmon of Ohio. Even perennial loser William Jennings Bryan was mentioned as a possible candidate.

Wilson was new to politics. He had won his first election two years earlier when New Jersey voters chose him as governor. His push for reform pleased many around the country, but it alarmed conservative voters in Florida. Florida would get to play a small role in the 1912 nomination process because it was about to have its first contested primary.

The preferred candidate in the South was Underwood, whose views on everything from race to the role of the federal government meshed nicely with those of Florida voters. The state primary had been created in 1904, but party officials considered it optional. In 1911 the Legislature clarified the law, and the first real primary was in 1912.

Although Underwood's popularity with voters was not surprising, what was surprising was that all seventeen of the state's daily newspapers lined up against him, some going to great lengths to criticize him. Wilson clubs were organized in Pensacola, Miami, St. Augustine, Tampa, and Jacksonville. Wilson traveled to Florida in April 1912 and spoke to 2,200 people at the Duval Theater in Jacksonville. It was his only Florida appearance, combined with a vacation trip to the Sunshine State.

A major force in the upcoming campaign was Bryan, the three-time Democratic nominee and three-time loser. Bryan, who saw Underwood as a reactionary, launched a swing through the state. He wasn't for Wilson yet, but he spoke against Underwood and Harmon.

Harmon managed to be even more conservative than Underwood. Harmon's idea for reform was to reduce federal spending to the point that each American would pay $1 a year in taxes. (At the time, Americans paid an average of $11 a year per capita.) He had the support of Governor Albert Gilchrist and a number of the state's newspapers, including

*The Tampa Tribune* and *The Florida Times-Union.*

But the Underwood forces had a plan to win newspaper support: bribery. If newspapers printed a collection of articles favorable to Underwood, they would receive money. The state's weekly newspapers were soon overflowing with stories about Underwood. His forces pointed out that as speaker of the House of Representatives, Underwood had a major say in federal aid to Florida farmers. Gilchrist, who had been supporting Harmon, swung to Underwood.

Behind the scenes, however, something was happening inside the Democratic Party that would profoundly affect the outcome of the primary. In early April, an Underwood friend and supporter, Senator John Bankhead, traveled to Florida to meet with Will Price, head of the Florida Democratic Executive Committee. No one knows what went on at their private meeting, but when the dust cleared, Price ordered Harmon and Clark removed from the ballot. Two of the four top candidates were gone with no explanation. It was a clear violation of party laws, which required all known candidates to be on the primary ballot.

With his challengers gone, Underwood had smooth sailing. The state's newspapers rallied around his cause, praising Underwood and damning Wilson, often with lies. Wilson was labeled as anti-Catholic and anti-Semitic. Newspapers claimed he "smelled" of socialism. Even though Wilson was a native of Virginia, newspapers labeled Underwood as the only true Southern candidate.

On Election Day, Underwood won the primary with 28,343 votes; Wilson received 20,482. Underwood had carried the rural areas of Florida, while Wilson carried the cities, including Miami, Jacksonville, Pensacola, Tampa, St. Petersburg, and Orlando.

At the national convention in Baltimore, Clark, who had been kept off the Florida ballot, led with 440 votes on the first ballot. Wilson had 324, Harmon had 148, and Underwood, the Florida winner, had 117. Clark seemed to be gaining strength; then, in the ninth ballot, the New York political machine threw its support to him. The move nearly put him over the top, but it also angered Bryan, an opponent of the machine. He stepped in to endorse Wilson enthusiastically and give him the nomination.

# Wilson's War with Western Union

The United States had been victorious in World War I, but in 1920 it faced a new, unlikely enemy: Western Union. The issue was a new telegraph line from Brazil to Miami. *The Miami Herald* was a major supporter of the telegraph line, which would open up new avenues of trade for south Florida. The problem began when Western Union decided to build a cable from Miami to Barbados Island and then connect to a British-owned line to Brazil. The British had cable rights in Brazil, which had denied American companies the right to land a cable there.

President Wilson wanted no part of it. He instructed his secretary of state to tell the British government that trying to land a cable in Miami would be "extremely inadvisable." But Western Union decided to ignore Wilson. In July a British cable ship arrived to connect a cable to another line extending just beyond the three-mile limit. Wilson dispatched four destroyers to Biscayne Bay and soon halted the cable hookup.

The company went to court and won victories over Wilson in two courts. The case then headed for the Supreme Court, which would not hear it until 1921. President Wilson's term had ended, and Western Union thought Republican President Warren G. Harding would allow the cable to go through. The company sent the *Robert Clowery* to link the cable to the shore, assuming the United States would do nothing. But the navy remained on guard in Biscayne Bay.

A submarine chaser was quickly dispatched to the *Clowery*. The chaser raised warning flags, but the crew ignored the warning and kept installing the cable. The navy ship finally fired a warning shot across the bow of the *Clowery*. The crew stopped work and headed toward shore, where they were arrested along with their captain. (They were soon released.) The Supreme Court finally ruled in favor of Western Union, and the cable link was completed. The Battle of Biscayne Bay was over, and a *Miami Herald* editor labeled it "just a tempest in a teapot."

## Wilson County? Well, Not Quite

Woodrow Wilson almost had a county in Florida named for him, but the honor ended up going to someone else. The story begins in 1925 when the residents of western Alachua County disagreed with residents in the eastern part of the county over several issues. Western residents wanted a new road built from the western part of the county to Gainesville, the county seat and home of the University of Florida. County commissioners rejected the road, however. Westerners were also against proposed laws requiring cattle to be fenced and disputed the division of race-track revenue. They started a petition drive to form their own county, and in late 1925, the Florida Legislature created one—the last and smallest of Florida's sixty-seven counties.

Florida was undergoing record growth, and new counties popped up frequently. Coming up with names had been a challenge. The leaders of the new-county movement had a name in mind, Melon County, in recognition of the watermelons grown in the area. But the legislature suggested naming the new county after former President Woodrow Wilson, who had died the year before. Then word arrived that former Governor Albert Gilchrist was ill in a New York hospital. The legislature thought it would cheer him up to give him an honor He died in 1926, leaving a large estate, mostly to charities. He also set aside money to buy ice cream for the children of his hometown, Punta Gorda, every Halloween. What would have been Wilson County became Gilchrist County.

# CHAPTER TWENTY-FOUR

# Warren G. Harding
## A Playful President Finds Fun in Florida

In 1920 Democrats faced a united Republican Party without an incumbent to boost their chances. The nation longed for change after eight years of Woodrow Wilson, World War I, and the ongoing debate over the League of Nations. The Republicans chose Senator Warren G. Harding, a former newspaper publisher. The Democrats chose another journalist, newspaper publisher James Cox of Ohio. Eugene Debs, the Socialist candidate, received nearly a million votes. In Florida, Cox got 90,515 votes, but Harding received 44,853, nearly three times what fellow Republican Charles Evans Hughes polled in 1916. In Florida, Debs received 5,189 votes, while Aaron Watkins, the Prohibition candidate, got 5,124 votes.

## A President-Elect Gets Stuck in the Mud

Before he became president, Harding was a regular visitor to Merritt Island and Daytona Beach. As president-elect, he spent two unplanned days in Titusville. Less than a month before being sworn in, Harding sailed up Mosquito Inlet on the yacht *Victoria*. But the inlet wasn't deep enough, and Harding's boat became stuck in the mud. During the stranding, Harding stayed mostly on the boat, but he left at one point to stretch his legs on the wharf at Titusville. He walked around, shook hands with residents, took a ride in what was called a "for hire" car, and bought mullet from a fisherman.

Harding returned two years later on the houseboat *Pioneer*, stopping in Rockledge, a short distance from Titusville, where he played golf. Harding complained of chest pains and difficulty breathing and asked his aide, Edmund Starling, "Why, after playing eleven or twelve holes, do I drag my feet and feel so tired?" Starling suggested he play fewer holes, but Harding replied, "Hell, if I can't play eighteen holes, I won't play at all."

While the president was visiting Cocoa Beach, developer Gus Edwards gave Harding and his wife the deed to an oceanfront lot and urged them to make the town their retirement home. Harding died later that year, however, and never developed the lot.

Warren Harding frequently wore a suit while fishing. (Photo courtesy of the State Archives of Florida)

## The Dream of the Florida White House Ends

The great showman John Ringling also hoped to convince President Harding to make Florida his home. He and his brothers had formed the Ringling Brothers Circus in 1870, later merging it with the Barnum & Bailey Circus while retaining control. John Ringling was only a child when his brothers first began their shows, and he learned the business as he grew up. He began visiting Sarasota in 1909 when it was a small town. His brother Alfred first brought the circus to Sarasota for the winter in 1919, and by the 1920s, the permanent winter headquarters was in Sarasota.

One of John Ringling's first jobs with the circus was as an advance agent, going from town to town to create interest in the upcoming performances. He was no less persistent when it came to promoting Sarasota. He began buying land in the town and on its outlying islands. He convinced John J. McGraw to bring his New York Giants baseball team to Sarasota for spring training, thus drawing thousands of Northern visitors, along with newspaper reporters who wrote about the town.

Some of the land Ringling purchased was on Bird Key, site of New Edzell Castle, which had been built by Thomas Worcester and his wife, Davidella "Davie" Lindsay Worcester. She was a descendant of the family that owned Edzell Castle in Scotland. The mansion took three years to build, and Mrs. Worcester died during construction. With her death, much of Worcester's joy for the property vanished. When he died in 1918, he left the home to his sister, who sold New Edzell Castle and all of Bird Key to John Ringling in 1922.

On neighboring St. Armands Key, a 150-acre island, Ringling named the streets after American presidents. At the center was Harding Circle. He offered the Edzell mansion to President Harding as a permanent winter White House. Ringling hoped Harding and future presidents would visit Sarasota, bringing national press coverage with them. Of course, many people eager to be neighbors of the president would buy land on Bird Key and Lido Key as well.

Ringling said that Harding liked the idea of a winter White House and was looking forward to an upcoming visit to Sarasota and a cruise on Ringling's yacht, the *Zalophus*. But the Harding administration was soon mired in scandal, and thoughts of a vacation faded. Instead, Harding headed west, ending up in California, where he died. The idea of the presidential home also died. In 1959 the Arvida Corporation purchased Bird Key and tore down the magnificent Edzell mansion to build the Bird Key Yacht Club.

## Harding Helps Promote a Booming Miami Beach

Like John Ringling, Carl Fisher hoped to use presidential sway to attract visitors to Florida. He is credited with opening the first automobile dealership, developing the Indianapolis Motor Speedway, and inventing the automobile headlight. He participated in the movement to involve the federal government in building highways, beginning with the east-west Lincoln Highway and then the north-south Dixie Highway. When the Dixie Highway was completed, Fisher celebrated his accomplishment with a drive from Indianapolis to Miami. It was there that he first saw the barrier island that he would transform into Miami Beach. In 1912 he built the Flamingo Hotel. After World War I, Florida underwent a huge land boom, and Miami Beach land suddenly soared in value. Often, land changed hands several times a day at ever-escalating prices.

Fisher attracted a growing number of wealthy people to south Florida, including tire king Harvey Firestone and retailer J.C. Penney. A master of publicity, Fisher had pictures taken of attractive women wearing bathing suits in winter, which he sent to newspapers in the frigid North. Fisher found his greatest publicity tool in Warren G. Harding. In early 1921, Harding visited Miami for a vacation before taking the oath of office.

D. C. 152—Flamingo Hotel, Miami Beach, Fla.

His original plan was to keep out of the public eye, but Fisher was determined to make sure that didn't happen. Harding arrived on a boat, planning to stay aboard. But waiting at the dock were

The Flamingo was the first resort hotel on Miami Beach and played host to President-elect Warren G. Harding. (Photo courtesy of the State Archives of Florida)

Fisher and his wife, Jane. Fisher took Harding to the penthouse of the Flamingo Hotel, where he had two of Harding's favorite things waiting: a poker game and a bottle of illegal Scotch whiskey. For the next week, the nation's newspapers covered Harding's every move in Miami Beach. The biggest stunt came when Harding played a round of golf. Photographers and reporters from around the country were on hand, but Fisher wasn't satisfied with simply having pictures of the president-elect playing golf. He wanted to create a moment everyone in America would be talking about. So Fisher obtained a small elephant to act as Harding's caddie. It worked. Sales soared.

President-elect Warren G. Harding uses an elephant as a caddie while golfing at the Flamingo Hotel in Miami Beach in 1921. (Photo courtesy of the State Archives of Florida)

# CHAPTER TWENTY-FIVE

# Calvin Coolidge
## A Regular Visitor to Florida

Warren G. Harding died in 1923, making his vice president, former Massachusetts Governor Calvin Coolidge, the next president. In 1924 Coolidge sought his own term and won easily, defeating Democrat John Davis of New York and Progressive candidate Robert LaFollette.

The city of Miami throws Calvin Coolidge a parade during one of his many visits to Florida. (Photo courtesy of the State Archives of Florida)

Coolidge received more than 15 million votes; Davis, 8 million; and LaFollette, nearly 5 million. In Florida the largely unknown Davis ran much stronger, receiving 60,083 votes, more than enough to beat Coolidge's 30,633 and LaFollette's 8,625. All of Davis's electoral votes came from the South, which remained loyal to the Democrats.

## Coolidge Found Relaxation in Mount Dora

In the 1920s, Florida was becoming the winter home to successful Northerners who built homes throughout the state. Calvin Coolidge visited Florida frequently as vice president, as president, and as a former president, usually to visit old friends and relatives from New England.

In 1929, as his term was coming to an end, Coolidge traveled to Florida to dedicate the Bok Tower at Lake Wales. Edward W. Bok, editor of the hugely popular *Ladies' Home Journal*, fell in love with the area around Lake Wales and in 1921 began building gardens to create a bird sanctuary. One of Coolidge's final acts as president was to dedicate its centerpiece.

On his way to dedicate Bok Tower in Lake Wales, Calvin Coolidge is welcomed to Winter Haven by the Citrus Queen. (Photo courtesy of the State Archives of Florida)

After his term ended, Coolidge returned to Florida to spend a month at the Lakeside Inn in Mount Dora. Built in 1883 as the Alexander Hotel on the shores of Lake Dora, it became one of the most popular resorts in the state. Marie Edgerton, whose family owned the inn from 1924 to 1979, remembered that Coolidge lacked a sense of humor but "Mrs. Coolidge (Grace) was a warm, friendly, loving person." Although he largely avoided speeches and publicity during his stay, the former president was pressed into service by the Edgertons to dedicate their new building.

At the end of Coolidge's Mount Dora visit, his cousin drove from Orlando to collect Coolidge and Grace. They had dinner with a relative of Mrs. Coolidge at a downtown Orlando home and spent the night there. The next day, they went to Sanford, where Coolidge received fresh fruit from the Florida Citrus Growers Clearing House Association and then traveled to Winter Park, where hundreds of people gathered to welcome him.

## The Famous Fraudulent Presidential Photograph

Coolidge was involved in an early case of doctored photographs. He attended the 1929 dedication of the "Senator," a 3,500-year-old cypress tree in a park south of Sanford. A picture of Coolidge and his wife standing in front of the tree was sent to newspapers all over the country and turned into postcards for souvenir seekers. It was a fraud, however. A picture of Coolidge and his wife had been superimposed on a picture of the huge tree. When the landmark caught fire and was destroyed in January 2012, the phony picture was again circulated.

## Murphree for President?

Virginia calls itself the "mother of Presidents," and even Hawaii has contributed a president to the nation. Florida, however, has never produced a president—or even a vice president—in more than one and a half centuries of statehood. Albert A. Murphree's name is known today only to the students who live in the University of Florida dormitory named for him. But in 1924, Murphree became the first Floridian to be mentioned as a presidential candidate, although he was mentioned by only one person.

EX PRESIDENT and
MRS. CALVIN COOLIDGE       BIGTREE
BETWEEN LAKE MARY - LONGWOOD    FLA.

Although widely circulated, this picture of Grace and Calvin Coolidge was a fraud. An image of the couple was superimposed on a picture of a giant tree outside of Orlando known as the "Senator." (Photo courtesy of the State Archives of Florida)

Murphree was president of the University of Florida and a nationally respected educator in 1924 when William Jennings Bryan decided he would make an ideal candidate for president. Bryan had been the Democratic presidential nominee in 1896, 1900, and 1908 and a candidate in 1912. In that last campaign, he threw his support to Woodrow Wilson, who rewarded Bryan by naming him secretary of state.

In 1912 Bryan purchased a winter home in Miami, and in the 1920s he became the spokesman for the new community of Coral Gables. Bryan had become famous for making political speeches; now he became wealthy by giving speeches to prospective land buyers. He spoke frequently at the University of Florida, where he met Murphree. Bryan told Murphree that he would make a great president. Although Murphree said he had no interest in a political career, Bryan kept pushing.

In early 1924, Bryan announced his candidacy as a convention delegate from Florida. He said he was running only so he could nominate Murphree for president, even though he hadn't consulted Murphree. Any candidate Bryan supported would receive national attention; soon newspapers throughout the nation carried stories about Murphree. But Murphree was realistic when he said, "Nobody expects a Southern man to be nominated president, much less a Florida man."

Bryan didn't back off and instead increased his efforts for Murphree. Bryan had grown out of touch with the National Democratic Party and failed to realize there was no way his friend could be the nominee. When Bryan nominated Murphree, delegates at the convention booed and heckled him. When the voting began, the clear winner was John Davis of New York. Murphree received just four votes, although a future president, Franklin Roosevelt, got only two votes. Bryan could take one consolation from the convention, however: His brother, Charles, was nominated for vice president.

# CHAPTER TWENTY-SIX

# Herbert Hoover
## A Presidential Fish Story

When Calvin Coolidge decided not to seek reelection in 1928, the Republicans turned to Herbert Hoover, who was a mining engineer, self-made millionaire, and secretary of commerce under Presidents Harding and Coolidge. For Southerners, Democrats chose the worst candidate possible: New York Governor Al Smith. Although the South had remained loyal to the Democrats no matter whom they nominated, Smith faced a serious challenge. First, he was Catholic in a region where anti-Catholicism was strong. He also favored the repeal of Prohibition in a region that had overwhelmingly supported outlawing the sale of liquor. Throughout Florida, ministers urged their parishioners to vote against Smith, even if it meant breaking with the Democratic Party and voting for the dreaded Republicans.

After the Civil War, the Republican Party seized political control of the Southern states and held it through Reconstruction. By 1880 the Democrats had swept the Republicans from power, giving birth to the Solid South. Republican presidential candidates had no chance of winning in Florida. In the twelve elections from 1880 to 1924, the Democratic presidential candidates easily won Florida. Then came Herbert Hoover and the election of 1928.

For the nation, the Great Depression was just around the corner, but in Florida, bad times had already begun. Banks were failing, land prices were collapsing, and the state was nearly broke. Hurricanes had ravaged the state, and even the state's major railroad, the Florida East Coast Railway, was on its way to bankruptcy. Florida voters were ready for change.

Problems for the Democrats began in Houston, Texas, where the party held the convention that nominated Al Smith. The Florida delegation opposed Smith. Fred Cone, a convention delegate who later became governor, was asked to serve on a committee to officially notify Smith that he had been nominated. To show his dislike for Smith, Cone created a minor stir when he declined to serve on the committee.

Methodist Bishop James Cannon organized southern Democrats into an anti-Smith movement. He arrived in Jacksonville in August, sponsored by the Anti-Saloon League, the Women's Christian Temperance Union, and local ministers. What was difficult to determine was whether the Protestant ministers battling Smith were upset primarily because of his opposition to Prohibition or his Catholicism. One reporter noted that Smith's Catholicism was rarely mentioned, but it was a major issue.

The state's Democratic Party found itself in uncharted waters. Its presidential candidates always won with no effort by the state party. In 1928 the party brought in politicians from other Southern states to beat the drum for Smith. The Democrats who supported Hoover became known as "Hoovercrats" and formed clubs throughout the state. The campaign soon became one of the nastiest in the state's history. As an olive branch to the South, the party had nominated Senator Joe Robinson of Arkansas for vice president, but when he spoke in Florida, people in the crowd heckled him and chanted, "Hurray for Hoover!" When former Democratic Governor Sidney Catts tried to speak on behalf of Smith in Gainesville, there was nearly a riot. The *Gainesville Evening News* reported that Catts "was forced to forego his speech because of hooting and throwing of eggs, one of which struck Catts squarely in the face."

The Florida Democrats seemed not to worry about the Hoover fever sweeping the state until it was too late. The party had a full slate of state and local elections to worry about, but as pro-Hoover support grew, there was concern that it might affect the local races. In fact, the Democrats won the governorship with just 60 percent of the vote, far below the usual 70–80 percent.

Hoover carried Florida by a wide margin: 143,716 votes to 101,764 for Smith. Tennessee and North Carolina also abandoned the Democrats.

Four years later, in the midst of the Great Depression, Florida would return to the Democratic column. Hoover, who received 60 percent of Florida votes in 1928, got just 25 percent in 1932. It would be 1952 before a Republican presidential candidate would win in Florida again.

## Hoover Goes After Al Capone

No one will ever know exactly why Herbert Hoover declared war on gangster Al Capone. Two stories have circulated for the past eighty years. Both stories begin in late 1928 following Hoover's overwhelming election as president. He decided to vacation in Florida to recuperate from the rigors of the campaign. J.C. Penney invited Hoover to be his guest in his mansion on Belle Isle, one of the islands between Miami and Miami Beach. Capone had a home on nearby Palm Island.

The first story is that Hoover's vacation was disturbed by noise and shooting coming from the Capone compound. According to the tale, Hoover vowed then and there to commit the federal government to putting Capone in prison. The second story is that, during the same vacation, Hoover was supposedly in a hotel lobby, talking to reporters. Capone entered the lobby and the reporters immediately rushed to him, abandoning Hoover.

The problem is that either of these scenarios surely would have generated tremendous publicity. If guns had been fired from an island in Biscayne Bay while the president-elect was staying nearby or if the president-elect and the nation's top crime boss had been in the same hotel lobby, it would have been front-page news. But there were no such news stories.

Whatever the reason, shortly after Hoover took the oath of office, one of his first orders was for the Treasury Department to get Capone—not for the criminal acts for which he was well known but instead for tax evasion. The government's case wasn't strong, but Judge James Wilkerson was clearly under orders to obtain a conviction, at times overstepping legal ethics to do it. After Capone was convicted, Wilkerson was nominated to the Court of Appeals, and there were rumors that he had been promised a Supreme Court seat. But the controversy was so great over his handling of the Capone trial that he withdrew his nomination. After Capone was released from prison, he returned to his Palm Island home, where he died in 1947.

## For Hoover, the Attraction Was Fishing

Herbert Hoover was a regular visitor to Florida before, during, and after his presidency. He liked to camp, and his favorite activity was fishing: From 1947 to 1958, he held the record for the largest bonefish caught in Florida. He celebrated Thomas Edison's eighty-second birthday in Fort Myers with Henry Ford and Harvey Firestone. He introduced Mary Roberts Rinehart, one of the leading mystery writers of the time, to Useppa Island off the southwest Florida coast. In 1912 Barron Collier, who had made a fortune in advertising, bought the island and turned it into an exclusive resort for tarpon fishing. In addition to Hoover, it attracted such luminaries as Zane Grey, Teddy Roosevelt, and Shirley Temple. Hoover

Herbert Hoover (far left) visits the Fort Myers home of Thomas Edison. With him are Henry Ford, Edison, and Harvey Firestone. (Photo courtesy of the State Archives of Florida)

became a regular, always keeping his tie and jacket on. Those who went fishing with Hoover, the engineer who had built huge dams most of his life, said he would often put down his fishing rod and build little dams in the river with rocks from the riverbank.

Flooding around Lake Okeechobee in south Florida had always been a problem. Storm surges on the lake caused by hurricanes killed several hundred people in 1926 and perhaps another 2,500 in 1928, although the exact death toll will never be known. Hoover took a personal interest in controlling the flooding. He inspected the huge lake, and the U.S. Army Corps of Engineers undertook a project to build a dike to hold

Herbert Hoover stands aboard the presidential yacht *Sequoia* in Fernandina, Florida. (Photo courtesy of the State Archives of Florida)

back the water, one of the defining moments of his administration. After many improvements, the dike was completed after Hoover left the White House, and in 1961 the elderly former president attended the dedication of the Herbert Hoover Dike.

## A Shameful Chapter

After World War I, Congress voted to pay veterans a bonus but delayed payment. As the Great Depression worsened, veterans wanted their money. Nearly 60,000 went to Washington in what became known as the Bonus March. Veterans camped in the Anacostia section of Washington, within sight of the Capitol. They built lean-tos, hammered together crates, and erected tents. The Senate refused to give them their money, however.

Most of the veterans returned home, but many had no place to go and decided to remain in Washington. Hoover saw the demonstrators as a threat to the nation, possibly fomenting trouble. In the worst single decision of his administration, he ordered General Douglas McArthur to use the army to remove the remaining veterans from their shantytown. Armed with tear gas, soldiers on horseback charged, driving the veterans— many with their wives and children—from the camp. It was all caught on film and shown in theaters around the country. Even Hoover admitted the debacle had damaged his chance for reelection.

When the Roosevelt administration took office in 1933, officials wanted to help the veterans who had been driven from Anacostia. The vets were sent to the Florida Keys to build the overseas highway to Key West. A proposal to build a large, reinforced hurricane shelter to protect the veterans in the event of a storm was rejected as too expensive. Nearly seven hundred men were living in temporary tents on Lower and Upper Matecumbe Keys over the Labor Day weekend in 1935. A massive hurricane had been building in the Florida Straits, but forecasting at that time wasn't good, and there was little warning that one of the deadliest storms of the century was on its way.

The men who had been forgotten so many times before were forgotten again. Officials at the camps knew about the storm, but many of the federal officials had taken off for the holiday weekend, and there was confusion about the rescue plan. The train sent to get the veterans off the Keys arrived during the heart of the storm and was swept from the tracks. The men tried desperately to seek safety, but there was no place to hide. At dawn, bodies were everywhere, even in trees. Many victims had been swept out to sea. The only good news was that several hundred veterans had left the camp earlier and gone to Miami for the weekend. The Labor Day hurricane of 1935 is still considered the most intense hurricane known to have struck the United States. The best estimates are that the winds at landfall in the Keys were around two hundred miles an hour.

The first reports to reach Washington said 252 veterans were dead or missing, but later estimates of the dead, including area residents, reached 500. At one camp, only 12 of 125 men survived. Roosevelt ordered that the veterans be identified and their bodies sent to their hometowns or to Miami for burial. But the rolls showing who was on the Keys were also destroyed in the storm, and many of the bodies were beyond identification. In the end, bodies were stacked like firewood and burned.

Newspaper editorials called the deaths a "national scandal" and a "colossal blunder" of the administration. The *Chicago Daily Tribune* said the hurricane might have been an act of God, but putting the veterans in harm's way was "a piece of criminal folly committed by someone in Washington." The newspaper asserted that the Florida camps had been set up to prevent another Bonus March in Washington and that the veterans had been sent to a remote area so people would forget them. Ernest Hemingway, a veteran himself, was living in the Keys at the time and wrote a scathing magazine article about the disaster, condemning the Roosevelt administration. An investigation by the American Legion blamed the tragedy on a combination of "inefficiency, indifference and ignorance" and concluded that the deaths were murder.

# CHAPTER TWENTY-SEVEN

# Franklin D. Roosevelt
## A Presidency that Nearly Ended in Florida

Franklin Roosevelt was on the ballot in Florida four times (five if you count his vice-presidential nomination in 1920), and Floridians gave him overwhelming majorities each time. In 1928 Hoover carried the state with 144,168 votes, but in 1932 more than half of his support faded away. Roosevelt, meanwhile, won more than double the number of votes earned by the 1928 Democratic candidate: He received 75 percent of the Florida vote. The Republicans' 1928 hope that their party had made permanent inroads in the South was an illusion. In 1936 Roosevelt faced a different candidate, Kansas Governor Alf Landon, but the result was the same. He actually did a bit better in Florida than in 1932, winning 76 percent of the vote. In 1940, as war raged in Europe and the nation turned its attention to foreign affairs, Roosevelt faced Wendell Willkie. Nationally, Roosevelt received just 55 percent of the vote this time, down slightly from his previous two bids for the White House. But Floridians remained faithful, giving him 74 percent of their votes. Roosevelt's winning percentage dropped to 70 in 1944, but in all four elections, he ran stronger in Florida than in the nation at large. In 1944 Florida's electoral vote count increased to eight.

## Roosevelt Comes Looking for a Cure in Florida

On August 10, 1921, Roosevelt was struck by poliomyelitis while visiting his summer home at Campobello Island in Canada. It is believed he became infected while visiting a Boy Scout encampment in New York a few weeks earlier. Roosevelt lost the use of his legs from the hips down. He began looking for a way to walk again, spending months with a doctor in Massachusetts, trying exercise routines, and cruising in south Florida on his family boat, the *Larooco*. He hoped that swimming in the warm waters around Florida would help him, but although he felt better, there was no lasting improvement in his condition.

The warm waters weren't the only attraction for Roosevelt. There was also his young secretary, Marguerite "Missy" LeHand. She went to work for Roosevelt in 1920; what began as a professional relationship became a friendship and then a romance. She accompanied him on voyages of the *Larooco*, playing the roles of secretary, hostess, and romantic interest. They returned to south Florida several times, the final time in 1926. Roosevelt became disenchanted with the swimming conditions, complaining, "The sharks made it impossible to play around in the deep water for any length of time." He had the *Larooco* stored at the Pilkington Yacht Basin on the Fort Lauderdale River and put it up for sale. But before there was any activity, a massive hurricane struck the coast and sent the boat up the river and inland. It ended up in a pine forest a mile from the river. Roosevelt then advertised the boat as a hunting lodge and tried to sell it once more. But in the end, the vessel was scrapped.

Roosevelt's trips to Florida left him feeling much better, and friends said he returned to New York looking younger. But the hectic pace of New York quickly tired him, and the improvement didn't last long. A friend suggested that he visit a run-down resort in Warm Springs, Georgia. Roosevelt found the rich mineral waters so buoyant that he could walk around the pool without his braces. He later purchased the entire resort and became a constant visitor.

## A Crazed Killer Takes Aim at Roosevelt

When he first visited Florida in the mid-1920s, Roosevelt held no political office. In 1928 he was elected governor of New York, and in 1932 he rode a wave of anti-Republican fervor to the White House. Before taking the oath of office in March 1933, Roosevelt headed to Florida for a vacation. He spent twelve days cruising off the coast on Vincent

Astor's yacht, the *Nourmahal*. The plan was for Roosevelt to make a brief appearance in Miami on his way to the train to take him back to New York.

At the same time, Chicago Mayor Anton Cermak was vacationing in Miami, seeking a break from the brutal Chicago winter. Cermak arranged a meeting with Roosevelt for two vital reasons. First, Cermak had not supported Roosevelt for the Democratic nomination and now wanted to get back in his good graces. Second, Chicago was broke and needed federal money to pay city workers, and only Roosevelt could deliver. On February 15, 1933, Roosevelt headed to Bayfront Park, where a large crowd was waiting. A platform had been set up, even though Roosevelt planned to address the crowd from his open car. When Roosevelt saw Cermak on the platform, he motioned for him to come down. Cermak shook his head and said he would join the president-elect after the speech.

At 9:30 P.M., Roosevelt made one of his shortest speeches ever—just 143 words. Cermak left the platform and walked to Roosevelt's car for a brief conversation. Standing nearby was Giuseppe Zangara, a mentally troubled man who had emigrated from Italy in 1923. As the crowd began to leave, Zangara stepped onto a chair, pulled out his $8 pistol, and opened fire. Mrs. W. H. Cross, the wife of a doctor, had been jostled by Zangara as he pushed his way to the chair and had grabbed his arm, spoiling his aim. He fired wildly, hitting five people but not Roosevelt.

Secret Service agents rushed to surround Roosevelt's car. At first, Roosevelt thought someone was setting off firecrackers. Cermak said the bullet that hit him felt like a bolt of lightning. Roosevelt's car began to move forward, but Roosevelt ordered it stopped and had the seriously wounded Cermak placed inside the car. Roosevelt put his arm around the mayor and kept it there all the way to Jackson Memorial Hospital. Roosevelt stayed at the hospital until 2 A.M. and then returned to Astor's yacht. He left the next morning for New York. Cermak had been shot on the right side of his chest, but the bullet couldn't be removed. On March 6, two days after Roosevelt was inaugurated, Cermak died.

The crowd set upon Zangara after the shooting. Secret Service agents rescued the gunman, threw him into the trunk of a car, and delivered him to the Dade County Jail. Zangara maintained that he hated

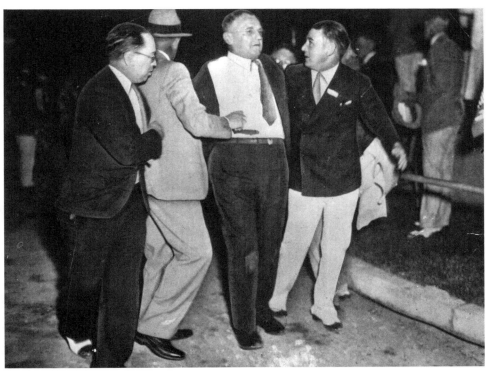

Chicago Mayor Anton Cermak is helped after being shot in Miami while talking to Franklin Roosevelt. (Photo courtesy of the State Archives of Florida)

all the world's rulers and that his stomach hurt. Before Cermak died, Zangara was convicted of multiple counts of attempted murder and sentenced to eighty years in prison. After the mayor's death, Zangara returned to court and this time was sentenced to death in the electric chair. Florida executed the gunman on March 20, 1933, just five weeks after the shooting.

Giuseppe Zangara is shown after being treated for injuries he suffered while trying to kill president-elect Franklin Roosevelt. (Photo courtesy of the State Archives of Florida)

## The Great Depression Hit Florida First

The Great Depression was well under way in Florida before it
reached the rest of the nation. Roosevelt's New Deal helped alleviate some
problems, but the economy in Florida remained weak until World War
II. Between 1929 and 1940, 157 state banks closed in Florida; another
45 national banks failed between 1925 and 1934. As Roosevelt took the
oath of office in 1933, one out of five Florida families required some type
of assistance. Before the year was out, the Civilian Conservation Corps
was active in Florida, planting millions of trees and putting thousands of
people to work. The Depression hit Key West particularly hard, and the
island's government declared bankruptcy. The federal government stepped
in to run the city and turned it into a resort destination. But despite a
tremendous influx of money from the federal government, it would take
World War II spending to bring the state back to prosperity.

Within weeks of the Japanese attack on Pearl Harbor, nearly every
part of Florida began a transformation. Even before Pearl Harbor, Florida
was playing a small role as President Roosevelt sought ways to help the
beleaguered British without bringing the United States into the war. A
major problem for the British was how and where to train pilots. It was
difficult to learn to fly in England with German fighter planes nearby.
Florida was perfect: It was flat, and the weather was good the entire year.
At first the British asked if they could use existing American pilot training
schools, but those were full of Americans who were anticipating a war.
America agreed to provide some small airfields if the British could find
instructors. One location was Carlstrom Field in Arcadia, which had been
abandoned for nearly fifteen years. John Riddle, who founded Embry-
Riddle College, launched a flying school for $500 and started a second
base in Clewiston. Six months before the Pearl Harbor attack, ninety-nine
British pilots arrived in Arcadia to begin training. In all, nearly 1,500
British pilots trained in Florida. About twenty-five pilots never returned
home: They were killed in training crashes and buried in a section of the
Arcadia cemetery. Every year, a memorial service is held to remember

them, and the British flag flies next to their tombstones.

By the end of the war, Florida had 172 military installations, including the massive Camp Blanding near Jacksonville, which became the fourth largest city in the state. The military took over hundreds of hotels to house soldiers, sailors, and pilots for training. Future president George H.W. Bush trained in Florida as a pilot.

Franklin Roosevelt arrives in Jacksonville during World War II on his way to south Florida. (Photo courtesy of the State Archives of Florida)

After Pearl Harbor, there were fears the Japanese might attack the West Coast. But the real threat was along the Florida coast. The Germans launched Operation Drumbeat to attack freighters carrying critical oil up the East Coast. One of Roosevelt's first orders of the war involved building boats to battle the German submarines lurking offshore.

## A Bridge and a President Salvage a Campaign

No doubt about it: Senator Claude Pepper was facing a tough reelection battle in 1944. He had made powerful enemies, including

Ed Ball, Florida's wealthiest and most powerful man. He had also taken political positions that had left him vulnerable. But Pepper had one huge fan, President Franklin Roosevelt. Pepper had been Roosevelt's strong Southern supporter, and Roosevelt desperately wanted to keep him in the Senate.

One of the strange things about Roosevelt's administration was that he faced constant problems with Southern senators, even though his greatest political support came from the South. Roosevelt made a number of unsuccessful attempts to get Southern voters to reject his opponents. If Pepper lost the Democratic primary, it would send a signal to opponents that Roosevelt's positions were losing popularity in the South.

Pepper did have several things going for him: He had done favors for thousands of people during his eight years in the Senate; he was the best-known politician in the state; and he had drawn a weak opponent. Ollie Edmunds was a Jacksonville judge with no political experience but a strong friendship with Ed Ball, whose wealth enabled him to dominate state government. Even though Edmunds was almost unknown and ran a poor campaign, Pepper was in trouble.

The Gandy family had no idea they would play a role in saving Pepper's political career. George Gandy had already made a fortune in the streetcar business in Philadelphia when he arrived in Florida in 1903 to explore installing a trolley line in St. Petersburg. He found there was no easy way to get from St. Petersburg to Tampa. Tampa Bay was in the way, and in the early 1900s, trips could take several days over the barely passable dirt roads that existed at the time. Gandy thought, Why not build a bridge to make the trip only a few minutes long?

Although his idea became known as Gandy's Folly, construction began on the bridge in 1918. He faced plenty of opposition, primarily from the railroad, which wanted to build its own bridge, and he had trouble raising money. In 1924 the bridge was completed and opened by the governor. It proved to be a boon to both Tampa and St. Petersburg, and coming in the midst of the Florida land boom, it also helped land sales.

To pay for his bridge, Gandy had poured his own money into the project and sold stocks to local residents. To pay off the investors, the privately owned bridge charged a toll. By 1944 George Gandy was ninety-three and blind, but he was still being driven to his office every day. He had no idea his bridge would be the key in the Senate campaign that year.

Five days before the election, Roosevelt made a stunning announcement: The federal government was taking over the Gandy Bridge and eliminating the thirty-five-cent toll. Roosevelt said he was doing it as a war measure to make it easier for employees of war-related companies to get to work. Both Tampa and St. Petersburg went wild with excitement. Schools in St. Petersburg were even closed for the day. Pepper won the primary by just four thousand votes. Edmunds said the bridge announcement had killed his campaign.

Meanwhile, Gandy was not pleased that his private property had been seized by the government. He and his family went to court and were awarded $2.5 million. Six years later—with the Gandy Bridge an issue and without Roosevelt's support—Pepper lost.

## The Florida Canal: Yet Another Try

Franklin Roosevelt's New Deal gave new life to the Cross-Florida Barge Canal. Roosevelt saw it as a way to put people to work, though he never addressed the need or impact of the canal. In making assessments of projects, the Army Corps of Engineers usually included an economic statement, but in this case the Corps didn't include the usual rosy economic analysis. This was strictly a means to create jobs.

In 1935 Roosevelt approved $5 million to get the project under way; an additional $400,000 was found from work-relief funds. Over a century, various schemes had recommended building a canal from 8 feet to 35 feet deep, and the costs estimates varied wildly. Roosevelt's estimate was $143 million for a 30-foot-deep canal. Talk about the value of the canal faded, however, amid predictions of 30,000 jobs created.

On September 19, 1935, Roosevelt was at his Hyde Park home when he pressed a telegraph key mounted on a gold nugget, signaling the start of construction. As The *Jacksonville Journal* wrote, Roosevelt had "blasted his name into Florida history." But like previous attempts to begin construction, this was another false start. Three months later, the president stopped approving more money for such projects as the barge canal; rather, Congress had to appropriate the money.

The initial money ran out in the middle of 1936, and only a small amount of work had been done. The Florida Legislature had chipped in $1.5 million and put new taxes in place. A new report in 1936 supported construction, but this time at a depth of 35 feet, and in 1937 there was yet another report with new dimensions and a cost estimate of $184.47 million.

Meanwhile, criticism of the canal was growing stronger. South Florida residents believed the canal might destroy the economy there; railroads thought it would hurt business; and scientists began to question what might happen to the state's underground water supply if seawater poured in from the canal. In 1937 Michigan Senator Arthur H. Vandenberg came out in opposition to the canal and demanded an investigation into canal spending.

Roosevelt kept pushing, but nothing happened until World War II, when supporters got a whole new argument—national defense. Early in the war, oil tankers coming from Texas up Florida's east coast were easy targets for German submarines. A canal would make the trip shorter and safer. This time, however, it would be a 12-foot-deep canal for barge traffic—no oil tankers—at a cost of $44 million. On July 23, 1942, Roosevelt signed legislation restarting the project, but no money was appropriated. The canal slipped away once again. Twice, Roosevelt had launched the Cross-Florida Barge Canal, but despite his support, there was still no canal.

# CHAPTER TWENTY-EIGHT

# Harry S. Truman
## A Presidential Retreat in Key West

As 1948 began, President Harry Truman's popularity was on the decline. A popular line that year was, "To err is Truman." Most Americans saw a Republican victory in November. Truman was facing opposition from all sides. The Republicans fielded New York Governor Thomas Dewey, and the Democratic Party splintered badly: Henry Wallace, the former vice president, declared his candidacy and became a left-wing challenger, and Governor Strom Thurmond of South Carolina announced his candidacy, running on a racist platform that appealed to Southern voters. But Dewey ran a weak campaign, Truman ran a masterful one, and neither Thurmond nor Wallace was as strong as he had appeared at the start of the campaign. Truman did nearly as well as Roosevelt had done in 1944, and Dewey attracted fewer voters than he had four years earlier. Truman carried Florida, which surprised many. Thurmond carried South Carolina, Louisiana, Mississippi, and Alabama but not Georgia or Florida. In Florida, Truman received 281,988 votes, besting Dewey's 194,280, Thurmond's 89,755, and Wallace's 11,620.

## Truman Finds His Little White House

In late 1946, Truman took a sailing vacation to Bermuda, but it turned into a disaster. Rough seas left him seasick, and he soon developed a cold that lingered for weeks. Admiral Chester Nimitz had just returned to Washington from a visit to Key West, where he had inspected the fleet. He suggested that a trip to Key West might be the answer to Truman's lingering cold and exhaustion.

In November, Truman arrived and stayed a week. The next spring he was back again, and by 1948 the visits were getting longer, increasing from one week to three. His final visit as president came in March 1952. Truman spent a total of 175 days there during his 8 years in office. He returned six more times after leaving office, the last visit coming in 1969. He proclaimed that Key West was his second favorite place on Earth, the first being his hometown of Independence, Missouri.

Harry Truman relaxes with wife Bess and daughter Margaret on the lawn of the Key West Naval Station. Truman was a regular visitor to what became known as the Little White House. (Photo courtesy of the State Archives of Florida)

## A Florida Senator Challenges a President

In Florida, Truman had a particular problem with Senator Claude Pepper, a fellow Democrat. Both had arrived in the Senate during the Great Depression as supporters of the New Deal. They sat next to each other in the Senate, but there was no friendship. Truman recalled that once, while he was giving a national radio address at a ship dedication in Bath, Maine, Pepper tried to take the microphone from him. In 1944 Pepper had tried unsuccessfully to deny Truman the vice-presidential nomination.

Truman should have been able to count on Pepper's support in 1948, but for three years before the election, Pepper hinted that he might support Henry Wallace or perhaps another candidate. In the weeks leading up to the Democratic National Convention in Philadelphia, Pepper became one of the leaders of the movement to deny Truman the nomination. The anti-Truman group went looking for someone to oppose the president—Dwight Eisenhower and Supreme Court Justice William Douglas were approached—but the president's foes came up empty-handed.

Finally, Pepper declared his own candidacy, claiming he had support from enough delegates to deny Truman the nomination. He actually had fewer than a dozen supporters. His candidacy was treated as a joke by nearly everyone. The *New York Times* called the Pepper announcement the funniest part of the convention, and newspapers in Florida were quick to criticize Pepper as well. The *Miami Daily News* said, "Senator Pepper is not a proper candidate for the Democratic party." Pepper's presidential candidacy lasted exactly one day. He was nearly laughed out of the race. Truman wrote to a Tampa friend that "the antics of one of the Florida Senators are right in line with what he usually does at every convention. He is merely a publicity hound."

Truman won the nomination and shocked everyone with a victory over Dewey in November. But he remembered Pepper's machinations and plotted his revenge. In 1946 Miami voters had elected George Smathers to Congress. Hailing from a wealthy family, Smathers had led a charmed life. Movie-star handsome, he had been an honor student at the University of Florida and played football and basketball. He served in the Marines and then resumed his job as an assistant United States attorney. He easily won reelection and in 1948 endeared himself to Truman by actively supporting the embattled president. The *Miami Daily News* commented, "Representative Smathers can have virtually anything he wants in the House. As long as Mr. Truman is in the White House, the door will always be open to him."

Truman began to invite Smathers to join him at the Little White House in Key West, and the two developed a warm friendship. In August

1949, Truman was ready to implement his plan for revenge. He invited Smathers to the White House and didn't mince words. Smathers said he told him, "Go down to Florida … make a survey and report" on the upcoming Senate election. Smathers also remembered Truman telling him to go out and defeat "that son of a bitch Claude Pepper."

Smathers had already been thinking about challenging Pepper, but the conversation with Truman provided him with more than encouragement. He knew Truman and the Democratic Party would do nothing to help Pepper win renomination. In both 1938 and 1944, the White House had been a key factor in helping Pepper keep his seat.

Smathers ran an effective campaign, while Pepper was hampered by many of his past actions. Pepper's supporters kept waiting for the Truman administration to help him, not knowing the president secretly supported Smathers. After he lost, Pepper said Truman bore part of the blame. Pepper's view was far different from that of anyone else involved in the election. He wrote, "The President told me some time ago that that he wanted me to win and did what he could to help me without sticking

Harry Truman rides through Key West following his defeat of Thomas Dewey in 1948. (Photo courtesy of the State Archives of Florida)

his neck out. They didn't do much, if anything—a rather sad commentary upon the faithfulness with which I have supported the administration." Pepper thought he had been faithful to Truman despite trying to deny him both the vice presidency and the presidency. Truman had had his revenge.

## The Space Age Comes to Florida

At the end of World War II, the missile range operating at White Sands, New Mexico, ran into problems, and it fell to President Harry Truman to create a solution. White Sands was thought to be too close to populated areas, and the range was just 135 miles long. In 1947 a rocket fired from White Sands was supposed to head north but instead went in the opposite direction and crashed in Juarez, Mexico, landing, ironically, in a cemetery.

A committee was established to consider better sites. Three emerged: the coast of Washington State; El Centro, California; and the Banana River Naval Air Station in Florida (with launches from Cape Canaveral). Initially, the California site won, Florida finishing second. But Mexican President Miguel Aleman objected to putting the range in El Centro, pointing to the proximity to populated areas in Mexico and the Juarez crash. On May 11, 1949, Truman signed legislation establishing the Long-Range Proving Ground at Cape Canaveral. The government already owned large pieces of land in the area, including the Cape Canaveral Lighthouse, and began buying up more land. From this modest beginning came the American space program.

## The Florida Canal: One More Try

As a United States Senator, Harry Truman had been a major supporter of a canal across Florida, even appearing in a pro-canal film produced to stir up interest in building it: "I think the canal should be built, and I hope that Congress makes the necessary appropriation for its construction." But when Truman became president in 1945, he was noncommittal, telling Florida Senator Charles Andrews, "I sincerely hope that eventually we can get it through." Hardly a battle cry for action. A year later, he wrote that he hoped the canal "may come about sometime in the near future."

But little was happening. In 1951 Truman wrote, "I've always been of the opinion that this canal is essential to the welfare of the country. . . . Although my judgment is not final on it." That year, Charles Bennett was the new congressman from Jacksonville, and over the next quarter century he became the canal's champion. He met with Truman at the White House and was convincing enough that Truman ordered another survey.

The Cold War presented a new opportunity for canal supporters, who said the project would help make the nation safer. But the Department of Defense threw cold water on that claim: "The military aspects of the proposed problem are so limited that they should not be used as the primary basis for decision on this matter." Once again, hope for the canal faded. Truman left office in 1953 and was replaced by Dwight Eisenhower, who displayed no interest in the canal whatsoever.

# CHAPTER TWENTY-NINE

# *Dwight D. Eisenhower*
## *A Healthy Trip to Florida*

Dwight Eisenhower revived the Republican Party in Florida. In every subsequent election, the Democrats could never again take the state for granted. After twenty years of Democratic rule, Florida was ready for a change. Eisenhower, the widely respected war hero, was the perfect nominee. His opponent was Illinois Governor Adlai Stevenson, who was not a strong campaigner. Eisenhower won by nearly seven million votes, the widest margin up to that point. Stevenson lost his home state and carried only most of the Southern states. In Florida, Eisenhower received 544,036 votes to Stevenson's 444,950. The state also added another two electoral votes to reach ten, making it an even bigger prize. In 1956 Eisenhower again ran against Stevenson, this time widening his lead to nearly nine million votes. Stevenson held only a swath of states from Virginia to Arkansas. Ike again took Florida, increasing his margin across the state.

## Recuperating—and Making News—in Florida

Twice, presidents have held news conferences in Florida that dominated the national news. Richard Nixon's is the better known. He gave his "I am not a crook" speech in Orlando in 1973. But a 1956 speech during the presidency of Dwight Eisenhower also went national.

In September 1955, Eisenhower was visiting the Denver home of his wife's family when he suffered a heart attack. He was taken to Fitzsimmons Veterans Hospital. In early 1956, he went to Key West to continue his recuperation. The big question the entire nation was asking was whether Eisenhower would seek a second term. He had not held a news conference since August 1955, before his illness, and the press kept pushing for answers. Finally, on January 6 at the Naval Station in Key West, he met with reporters. He began by making light of the situation: "The press secretary has told me there has been some curiosity about the sojourn here in Key West and its effect on me. . . . The whole experience has been a pleasant one."

Eisenhower went on to discuss the farm program and the upcoming State of the Union address, but the reporters had only one thing on their minds. United Press reporter Merriman Smith asked, "Mister President, are you . . . will you entertain some questions about your political future?"

Eisenhower was evasive. "Well, I think, Mister Smith, there would be very little reason or very little, you might say, benefit . . . value in discussing it this morning."

Bob Clark of the International News Service kept pushing: "Mister President, does that mean, as of this moment, you have not made up your mind as to whether you will run for a second term?"

Eisenhower replied, "It means, as of this moment, I have not made up my mind to make any announcement as of this moment."

The reporters laughed. There were more questions, all on the same subject, but Eisenhower sidestepped each one. Finally, on February 29, 1956, he announced his candidacy for a second term. He was reelected by a wide margin in November.

# CHAPTER THIRTY

# John F. Kennedy
## A Home Away from the White House

The 1960 election featured two men who knew Florida well. John Kennedy's family had a home in Palm Beach, and he had been a frequent visitor since his youth. Richard Nixon had been visiting since his election to the Senate in 1950. The Republican Party was becoming stronger in Florida and throughout the South, and Nixon made an effort to appeal to Southern voters. Nationally, the election was razor-thin, with Kennedy receiving 34,220,984 votes to 34,108,157 for Nixon. Kennedy had a more comfortable lead in the electoral vote; still, a shift of 50,000 votes would have given the election to Nixon. The Florida vote was also close, but Nixon was the winner, receiving 795,476 votes to Kennedy's 748,700.

### New Wealth and a New Palm Beach Home

Florida was the fastest-growing state in the nation during the 1920s. An influx of wealthy Northerners settled an area from Palm Beach to Miami that became known as the state's Gold Coast. Henry Flagler had started drawing his wealthy friends to Florida with a grand hotel in St. Augustine and then worked his way south, building hotels and a railroad along the way. Eventually, he reached Key West, but the island of Palm Beach was his master creation. There were actually two towns: Palm Beach for the very wealthy and West Palm Beach for the railroad workers and the staff who served the wealthy on Palm Beach. The two were separated by a body of water that protected the privacy of the island residents.

If Palm Beach was the place to live, then Addison Mizner was the architect to build that place. Mizner was forty-six when he moved to Palm Beach for his health. He found a willing clientele for his sprawling homes, which combined his Mediterranean Revival style with adaptations to Florida's hot summers. His homes were generally one room deep to allow for cross ventilation. Built of stone, stucco, and tile, they became a huge success.

In 1923 Mizner designed La Guerida ("Bounty of War") for Rodman Wanamaker, the Philadelphia department store tycoon. Wanamaker's health soon declined, and he died in 1928 of kidney disease. His children held the home for several years and then sold it in 1933 for $120,000 to Joseph P. Kennedy, who added another wing and a tennis court for his large family. John F. Kennedy, a teenager when the home was purchased, was a frequent visitor to the house. It wasn't until 1954, however, that he spent an extensive amount of time there. Beginning in 1938, Kennedy had serious problems with his back. Surgery in 1954 nearly killed

John Kennedy has his portrait painted by Elaine de Kooning as he talks to Agriculture Secretary Orville Freeman in Palm Beach. (Photo courtesy of the State Archives of Florida)

him, and he spent much of his eight-month-long recovery at La Guerida. (The Kennedy family asked the physicians who performed the surgery to destroy the medical files.) During his recuperation, he worked on *Profiles in Courage*, which won the Pulitzer Prize, although we now know it was largely written by his aide, Theodore Sorensen.

Kennedy's parents spent the 1960 election night at the Palm Beach home and watched as the returns brought news that their son had been elected president. Kennedy was in Massachusetts to watch the vote count, but he soon arrived in Florida to rest and assemble his Cabinet. He held press conferences on the patio to announce administration appointments.

## An Almost-Forgotten Assassination Plot

On December 16, 1960, two airplanes crashed over New York City. A United Airlines flight approaching Idlewild Airport (now John F. Kennedy International) with eighty-four passengers slammed into a Trans World Airlines flight heading for LaGuardia Airport from Columbus, Ohio. The crash killed 128 people on the two planes and 6 more on the ground in Brooklyn. Viewers across the country watched the smoky ruins of the two planes on the nightly news. Had it not been for that plane crash, a story occurring about one thousand miles away might have dominated the news.

Instead, the case of Richard Pavlick became a historical footnote. The seventy-three-year-old Pavlick was well known to the Secret Service because he had been writing threatening notes to presidents for years. On Sunday, December 11, Kennedy left his Palm Beach home for church services. Pavlick parked near the front gate of the compound on a side street, his car loaded with dynamite. His plan was to drive his car into Kennedy's limousine and set off an explosion, but he changed his mind when he saw Kennedy's wife, Jackie, come through the gate with him. Pavlick later told authorities that he had no intention of killing Mrs. Kennedy.

Instead, he drove to St. Edward's Catholic Church, near the Kennedy compound, with a new plan of killing the president-elect there. Inside the church, a Secret Service agent sat behind Kennedy, and two other agents sat near the aisles. Agent Gerald Blaine was posted at the entrance. When Pavlick entered the church, he immediately caught the eye of Blaine, who thought the disheveled man looked out of place amid the well-dressed parishioners.

Pavlick headed down the center aisle toward Kennedy's pew, and Blaine left the door to follow Pavlick. As Pavlick drew closer, Blaine took his elbow and quietly pulled him back. As Blaine and coauthor Lisa McCubbin wrote in *The Kennedy Detail*, Blaine tightened his grip on Pavlick's arm and guided him toward the church entrance. Pavlick said Blaine's actions made him nervous, and he decided again to scrap his plan.

Pavlick left St. Edward's, got into his car, and drove off. Blaine wrote down the license plate number and a description of the car. The Palm Beach Police Department was notified to keep an eye out for the vehicle. Four days later, on December 15, Palm Beach police officer Lester Free saw Pavlick's 1950 Buick and stopped him. Inside, he found ten sticks of dynamite, wire, and a detonation device. Pavlick readily admitted that he wanted to kill Kennedy. He was committed to a mental hospital but released in 1966. He died in a Veterans Administration hospital in 1975.

## A Secret Service Agent Fires His Gun

The president wasn't the only Kennedy family member who faced a threat in Palm Beach. Secret Service agent Ed Tucker was in charge of guarding daughter Caroline Kennedy, but he had come down with the flu and was recovering nearby at Woody's Motel. Agent Lynn Meredith stepped in and took Caroline and her cousin, Christopher Lawford, to play at a Palm Beach playground.

Meredith said the children soon grew bored with the usual playground equipment and started exploring. They flipped over logs and under one of them found a large snake. The children screamed, and Meredith recognized the snake as a venomous Eastern diamondback rattlesnake. He drew his gun and fired twice, killing it. At the end of his shift, he returned to the motel, showed Tucker the discharged cartridges, and told him what had happened. "I'm probably going to be fired," Meredith told Tucker. "But it's better than trying to explain how Caroline got bitten by a rattlesnake." Caroline's nanny convinced the girl to keep the incident a secret, and it was not revealed until half a century later in a book.

## The Florida Canal: New Start, Same Outcome

The election of John Kennedy offered new hope to supporters of the 150-year-old idea to build a canal across Florida. Unlike Eisenhower, Kennedy supported public works projects, and with growing threats in Cuba, proponents could once again claim the canal was a military advantage. A large headline in *The Ocala Star Banner* said it all: "Kennedy Backs Florida Canal."

Just months after his inauguration, Kennedy asked for $195,000 for what he called final planning and initial construction. Kennedy predicted the canal would carry as much freight as the Suez Canal, and he pointed out the need to get rocket parts to Cape Canaveral. Boosters even proposed a second canal to link the main canal directly to the space center.

Despite the high-level support, little progress was made on the canal. The $195,000 Kennedy asked for got held up in Congress; when it finally emerged, the money could be used only for yet another study, not actual construction work. Backers of the canal were becoming better organized, however, and when Kennedy proposed another $205,000 for the project in 1961, they successfully lobbied for the money in Congress. Backers could claim some success, but as supporters had seen repeatedly for more than a century, a victory one day didn't mean a victory the next.

When Kennedy submitted his budget for 1963, the canal had disappeared. Florida supporters mounted a massive campaign to convince Kennedy to reinstate canal funding. They used every argument they could think of, including suggestions that if Kennedy hoped to carry Florida in 1964—he had not carried it in 1960—he had better get behind the canal. Kennedy relented and asked Congress for $1 million for canal construction. The bill picked up steam and overwhelmingly passed Congress on November 20, 1963. Two days later, however, Kennedy was killed in Dallas, and yet another president inherited the canal.

# John Kennedy's Final Florida Visit

Kennedy visited Palm Beach frequently as president. On November 12, 1963, he held a high-level meeting in Washington with his senior political advisors, who determined that Florida and Texas were crucial to Kennedy's reelection the following year. On November 15, 1963, he flew to Palm Beach and went to Cape Canaveral the following day. Returning to Palm Beach, he worked on a speech and had a private screening of the new movie *Tom Jones*. He left Palm Beach for the final time on November 18 to make speeches in Tampa and Miami, and then returned to Washington before leaving for Texas on November 21.

John Kennedy and Senator George Smathers greet crowds in Miami just four days before Kennedy's death. (Photo courtesy of the State Archives of Florida)

In 1995 the Kennedy family sold La Guerida to a New York hedge fund executive and his wife. The Kennedys had asked $7 million for the property, but it sold for $4.9 million.

# CHAPTER THIRTY-ONE

# Lyndon B. Johnson
## Launching Florida into the Space Age

With the death of John Kennedy, Lyndon Johnson became president in 1963 and less than a year later ran for his own four-year term. For Johnson, it was never a question of victory but of margin of victory. There also was a question of whom the South would vote for in the election. Johnson had pushed civil rights legislation, which had alienated the traditional Democratic base in the South. Republican nominee Barry Goldwater, with his talk of states' rights, appealed directly to the South. Johnson won a massive victory, receiving 43,124,041 votes to just 27,175,754 for Goldwater. In Florida the vote was much closer: Johnson received 948,540 votes; Goldwater, 905,941. Goldwater's Southern strategy paid off with wins in Georgia, Mississippi, Alabama, Louisiana, and South Carolina, but Florida, thanks largely to massive immigration from the North, was no longer part of the Solid South. As a result of the 1960 census, Florida's electoral vote increased to fourteen, four more than in 1950.

The 1964 election brought a realization of the growing political strength of Florida Republicans in presidential races, even if the Democrats controlled nearly all the state offices. Florida voters had long chosen their governors in the same year as presidential elections. Florida Democrats realized that the popularity of Republican presidential candidates had the potential to swamp Democrats running for governor. So, beginning in 1966, gubernatorial elections were moved to off years. It didn't help. That year Florida voters elected the state's first Republican governor since Reconstruction and, in 1968, its first Republican senator since Reconstruction.

## The Florida Canal: Hope Springs Eternal

After Johnson took the oath of office on November 22, 1963, he quickly began pushing for a huge public works bill that included $1 million for construction of the Cross-Florida Barge Canal. He signed it before the year was out, and canal supporters saw another $4 million in 1964.

Not since Franklin Roosevelt had there been a president so committed to large public works projects. Roosevelt was Johnson's idol, and Johnson had seen the impact of such New Deal projects as the Tennessee Valley Authority, which brought electricity to millions. The canal was just the type of massive project that appealed to Johnson.

On February 27, 1964, more than 10,000 people turned out at a ranch near the small town of Palatka to see President Johnson pull a bright red switch and set off 150 pounds of dynamite. The weather that day was

Senator Lyndon Johnson, second from right, fished in south Florida with Senator George Smathers, far left, and other senators. Behind them is Bebe Rebozo, who was also Richard Nixon's best friend. (Photo courtesy of the State Archives of Florida)

miserable, and Johnson gave his speech in a driving rain. It was yet another start for the canal, but it ended up no more successful than the others.

The canal builders were working off a 1943 War Department proposal for a waterway 12 feet deep and 150 feet wide. The canal would serve barges but not large ships that needed deeper water. Still, that was at least something after nearly 150 years of waiting.

Construction began, but it went slowly. Members of the Interior Department thought that at the rate things were going, the project could take decades to finish. They took many things into consideration, and one new factor was a growing environmental movement, which increasingly challenged the canal.

Meanwhile, another problem was developing half a world away. For decades, supporters of the canal had used national defense as a reason to build it. Now national defense was a threat to the project. The escalating war in Vietnam was draining money from the Army Corps of Engineers. In 1968 the canal received just half the money requested to continue construction. Johnson, desperate to spend for both a war and his "Great Society" without increasing taxes, froze public works expenditures. Although the original plan was to finish the canal in 1970, it now appeared it could take years—maybe a decade or more.

Johnson, who had come into office as the champion of the canal, left office after slashing spending for it. As historians Steven Noll and David Tegeder have pointed out, the "canal was part of the patchwork quilt of modern liberalism that began to fray in the 1960s. Created as a New Deal work project, and later resurrected amid talk of new frontiers, the barge canal also represented the expansive vision of Johnson's Great Society."

The canal was passed on to yet another president.

## Johnson Creates the Space Race

When people think of presidents and the space program, they usually remember John Kennedy and his pledge to put a man on the moon in the 1960s. But if the space program has a father, it is Lyndon Johnson, whose involvement began as a case of political opportunism.

In 1957 the Russians launched Sputnik 1, a sphere of aluminum that emitted radio signals. President Eisenhower was pleased with the news: Now that the Russians had launched a spy satellite, the United States could go ahead with its plans without worrying about diplomatic fallout.

Lyndon Johnson was the Senate majority leader, gearing up for a presidential campaign in 1960. An aide suggested that the launch of the Russian satellite could be turned into a political issue to help the Democrats and embarrass the Republicans. Not only could the Republicans be made to look as though they were giving a military advantage to the Russians, but Democrats, by calling for space exploration, could also appear to be the party of the future.

Johnson called for Senate hearings, saying he wanted to know why the Russians had gotten ahead of us, even though they weren't really ahead of us. The hearings lasted six weeks, and even before they were over, the words "space race" had entered the national vocabulary. Johnson introduced and pushed through the National Aeronautics and Space Act of 1958, setting off events leading to the moon landing eleven years later.

Johnson ended up with the 1960 vice-presidential nomination, but the presidential nominee, John Kennedy, turned the "missile gap" into one of his major issues in the campaign. On April 25, 1961, after Kennedy moved to the White House, he signed legislation that made Johnson the head of the National Aeronautics and Space Council. Johnson supported Kennedy's plan—and may have been responsible for the idea—to put a man on the moon before the end of the 1960s.

Cape Canaveral's history as a space center began in 1949 when it was chosen as a testing site. Cape Canaveral was isolated, sparsely populated, and on the Atlantic Ocean: Unsuccessful launches would land harmlessly in the water. Lastly, it was closer to the equator than other sites being considered. By taking full advantage of the earth's rotation, launches required less fuel. Johnson's support of Cape Canaveral brought thousands of well-paying jobs and related industries to central Florida as the space program boomed. The federal government purchased land on Merritt Island to expand its facilities, and money poured into the region throughout the 1960s.

But Johnson also took action that sent the local economy into a tailspin after the moon landing in 1969. First, in his role as chairman of the National Aeronautics and Space Council, Johnson decided to establish a national headquarters for space programs. There were space-related facilities at Langley Air Force Base in Virginia, at Cape Canaveral, and in Huntsville, Alabama. Any of them could have been the headquarters. Johnson was from Texas, however, and he chose Houston. The bulk of the space jobs went there, including the home for the astronauts.

Second, although Johnson had been the prime instigator of space programs, his policies as president brought those programs nearly to a standstill after the triumphant moon landing in 1969. Johnson had launched his Great Society, a program to make life better for millions of Americans, and he had dramatically increased American involvement in Vietnam. Both of these objectives were extremely expensive, yet Johnson wanted to keep taxes down while spending freely. Cuts had to be made, and the space program was selected for a hit. Even as the nation celebrated the moon landing, layoffs were already planned for many of the Cape Canaveral workers who had made it possible. The space shuttle program brought back many of the jobs, but after Apollo and the move to Houston, things were never the same at Cape Canaveral.

## CHAPTER THIRTY-TWO

# Richard M. Nixon
## Finding a Home in Key Biscayne

Richard Nixon lost the 1960 presidential election by the narrowest of margins to John Kennedy. After losing the California governor's race two years later, his political career seemed to be over. But Nixon staged a remarkable comeback after the Republican collapse in 1964, winning his party's nomination four years later in Miami Beach. The Democratic Party was in disarray. Its presumed candidate, President Lyndon Johnson, had withdrawn; Senator Bobby Kennedy had been assassinated; Senator Eugene McCarthy had been weakened by the Kennedy candidacy; and the eventual nominee, Vice President Hubert Humphrey, had tremendous political baggage. Still, Humphrey came agonizingly close, receiving 31,271,839 votes to 31,783,783 for Nixon. Complicating the campaign was the candidacy of third-party candidate George Wallace, the racist Alabama governor who received nearly ten million votes. Wallace had no chance of winning, but he might get enough votes to throw the race into the House of Representatives. He carried the Deep South states of Arkansas, Louisiana, Alabama, Mississippi, and Georgia, and he placed second in Tennessee, North Carolina, and South Carolina. In Florida, Nixon won easily with 886,804 votes, compared to 676,794 for Humphrey and 624,207 for Wallace.

The results of the 1972 election were never in doubt. Both the Republicans and the Democrats held their conventions in Miami Beach, with the Democrats choosing George McGovern and the Republicans renominating Nixon. The president's appeal to the South was clear, and he racked up huge vote margins not seen in the South since the days of Franklin Roosevelt. In Florida he got nearly 70 percent of the vote. Florida's population surged again in the 1970 census, and the state gained three more electoral votes for a total of seventeen. The Sunshine State had become one of the top ten electoral prizes and began to figure more and more in the plans of presidential candidates.

## Richard Nixon: The Environmental President

When most Americans hear the name Richard Nixon, they think first of Watergate or other scandals or Vietnam. Few think of him as an environmentalist, but that's how many Floridians remember him.

Nixon took office in 1969 as environmental opponents of the Cross-Florida Barge Canal were becoming better organized and beginning to draw national attention. An article in *Reader's Digest* was particularly

Republican presidential nominee Richard Nixon, vice-presidential nominee Spiro Agnew, and their families mingle at the 1968 Republican National Convention in Miami Beach. (Photo courtesy of the State Archives of Florida)

antagonistic. The environmentalists decided to bring Nixon into the fray. In early 1970, 162 leading scientists signed a letter calling for Nixon to stop construction of the canal and halt a "major, national ecological disaster." The letter called the canal a waste of money and spoke of threats to the environment. Days before the letter appeared, Nixon had promised to protect the environment; the scientists sought to hold him to his word.

Nixon had already sided with environmentalists over one Florida issue, the Miami Jetport. The idea of a jetport had been born in the 1960s to ease congestion at Miami International Airport. Plans called for building the giant airport and a community for more than 100,000 people in the Big Cypress Swamp. As with the canal, however, opposition developed, spurred by environmentalists who said the jetport would cause widespread damage to the environment.

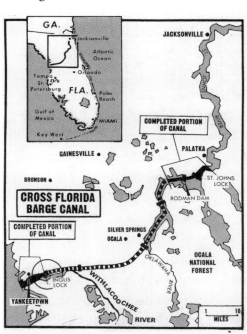

When Richard Nixon killed the Florida Canal, much work had already been done, but the ambitious plan was more than a decade from completion.

As opposition grew, the Nixon administration ordered a study of the environmental issues. The report came down clearly on the side of the jetport's foes. One year after becoming president, Nixon stepped in and the plan died, giving new strength to the environmentalists trying to stop the canal. They began to gain support from Nixon aides, who urged the president to halt the project. Secretary of the Interior Walter Hickel asked that construction be halted for fifteen months to allow more studies on the environmental consequences of building a canal.

In the fall of 1970, Richard Nixon arrived in Florida to campaign for Republican candidates. He told a crowd that "any program by the federal government . . . whether it is a barge canal or anything else, will not go into a place unless we are given assurance that it is not going to affect the environment." In mid-January 1971, the White House issued a brief statement with no fanfare. "I am today ordering a halt to further construction of the Cross-Florida Barge Canal to prevent potentially serious environmental damage," Nixon's statement said. "A natural treasure is involved in the case of the Barge Canal—the Oklawaha River, a uniquely beautiful, semitropical stream, one of the very few of its kind in the United States, which would be destroyed by construction of the canal."

Historians David Tegeder and Steven Noll discovered that Nixon's decision was nearly reversed later. In their book, *Ditch of Dreams*, the two recount that Nixon soon took a trip to Miami and visited his best friend, Charles "Bebe" Rebozo, who gave him an earful about the canal. Rebozo had spoken to Floridians—primarily Jacksonville businessmen—who were angry about the canal decision and wanted him to get Nixon to reconsider. On the flight back to Washington, Nixon told an aide he had changed his mind about the canal. The aide passed along Nixon's second thoughts to another aide, John Whitaker: "I sat on it and did nothing, hoping the storm would blow over," Whitaker recalled. A week later, Nixon asked for an update and was told nothing had happened. Nixon then agreed to stand by his original decision to halt canal construction. Nixon smiled and said, "Too bad. Jacksonville was a great town."

## Denying Being a Crook at Disney World

It was probably not the type of publicity Walt Disney World was looking for. On Sunday, November 18, 1973, hundreds of thousands of readers of *The New York Times* picked up the newspaper and read the lead story on the front page. The dateline was "Disney World, Fla.," but the story didn't deal with the rides or the entertainment.

Hundreds of journalists had come to Disney World in Orlando to cover a speech by President Richard Nixon to the Associated Press Managing Editors Convention at Disney's Contemporary Hotel. The nation was fixated on the Watergate scandal. In June 1972, burglars had been caught breaking into the offices of the Democratic National Committee at the Watergate office-residence complex in Washington. Nixon was vacationing at his home in Key Biscayne when the break-in occurred, and his press secretary said that the president wouldn't comment on a third-rate burglary. Nixon did his best to downplay the crime, but instead the story had grown.

Nixon and Disney had a long history together. In 1955, one month after Disneyland opened in California, Nixon, his wife, Patricia, and their two daughters visited the park. Fess Parker, who had played Davy Crockett on Disney's TV show, personally greeted the vice president and gave him the key to Disney's City Hall. Nixon's family lived near the park and became regular visitors, showing up dozens of times in the 1950s and 1960s. Nixon dedicated Disneyland's new monorail in 1969. The Orlando speech was his first visit to Florida's Disney World, which had opened in 1971.

During the 1972 presidential election, the Democratic candidate, George McGovern, had tried to make Watergate an issue with little success. But as the months went by, details began to emerge, linking the burglary to his reelection campaign. Nixon had done his best to dodge questions about Watergate, but at Disney World he faced journalists in a one-hour question-and-answer session. It was there that he uttered one of his most famous quotes: "I've made my mistakes, but in all of my years of public life, I have never profited—never profited—from public service. I've earned every cent," Nixon said. "And I think, too, that I can say, that in my years of public life, I welcome this kind of examination, because people have got to know whether or not their president is a crook. Well, I'm not a crook." Nixon also seemed to confirm a newspaper story that reported he had paid just $792 in taxes in 1970 and $878 in 1971. He said that he had simply taken the appropriate deductions.

The *Times* also described the scene at the Disney hotel where the president spoke. "The political importance of the occasion and the sober comportment of the editors were in sharp contrast to the setting. Mr. Nixon spoke in a gaudily modern room—blue draperies, orange chairs, mirrors on the ceiling—near the monorail line that passes through the hotel and leads to the 'Magic Kingdom.' "

Despite Nixon's denials, the details of Watergate continued to emerge. Ten months after he declared he was not a crook, Nixon resigned to avoid impeachment. He was later pardoned by his successor, Gerald Ford.

## A Florida Getaway Becomes a Florida White House

After his election to the United States Senate in 1950, Richard Nixon was exhausted. He had just gone through a grueling campaign against Helen Gahagan Douglas, the wife of actor Melvyn Douglas. He turned to his friend, George Smathers, another newly elected senator, for advice. Smathers and Nixon had come to the House of Representatives in 1947, part of a class of World War II veterans who had been born in the twentieth century and been tested in battle. One-fifth of the members of the 1947 Congress were World War II veterans.

Smathers was one of the most likable members of the new class, the child of a wealthy Miami family and a success at everything he tried. It was a marvel how he could make a friend of nearly anyone. For example, his two best friends in the new Congress were John Kennedy and Richard

Richard Nixon turned this Key Biscayne house into the Florida White House. (Photo courtesy of the State Archives of Florida)

Nixon, two very different men. Democrat Smathers had even given campaign advice to Nixon, a Republican. Smathers had also been a good friend of Harry Truman.

Smathers told Nixon that Key Biscayne was the perfect place for a getaway, namely the Key Biscayne Hotel and Club. He even recommended a friend who might show Nixon around, Bebe Rebozo. Nixon called Rebozo, who took Nixon deep-sea fishing on his thirty-three-foot Chris-Craft. Nixon hated fishing, however, and, according to Rebozo, couldn't bring himself to kill anything. Rebozo thought Nixon's visit was a failure, but Nixon did enjoy it. Key Biscayne became a getaway for Nixon for the next quarter century, and Rebozo also became his best friend. After losing the 1960 election, Nixon had his first meeting with president-elect Kennedy at the Key Biscayne Hotel.

After his election in 1968, Nixon began to assemble his Cabinet. There were rumors that as part of an effort to unify the nation, he might name a Democrat to a

After a 1950 visit to Key Biscayne, Richard Nixon became best friends with businessman Bebe Rebozo. (Photo courtesy of the State Archives of Florida)

Cabinet post. How better to do that, the speculation ran, than to select his friend George Smathers as attorney general? Smathers had been an assistant United States attorney before running for office. All that was needed was the call from Nixon. A call did come, but it was not what the Smathers family was expecting. Instead of a job offer, Nixon wanted a favor: Would Smathers sell his home in Key Biscayne to Nixon? Smathers said yes, the Smathers home became the Florida White House, and Smathers didn't become attorney general.

Key Biscayne had been developed by the Mackle family to provide affordable housing for World War II veterans in the early 1950s. The new houses were basic, cinder-block structures that were springing up everywhere in Florida. Each tract house cost $9,450 and was designed for a family starting out during the baby boom. The Smathers-Nixon house was certainly nothing special, but it was just what the new president wanted. Eventually, he came to own three homes on Key Biscayne and created his own compound. During his presidency, taxpayers paid $10.5 million for what were classified as security improvements, including a $400,000 floating helicopter pad, which played a small role in Brian De Palma's 1983 movie, *Scarface*. Nixon sold the Key Biscayne compound after leaving office. In 2004 the Nixon home was torn down to make way for one of the new mansions that became the rage when property values soared in Key Biscayne.

One thing that never changed was Rebozo's friendship with Nixon. When Rebozo opened his bank in 1964, Nixon arrived for the dedication. When Nixon bought his new house, Rebozo's bank helped with the financing. It is believed that after Nixon was forced to resign, he had some financial problems before making a small fortune. His old friend, Rebozo, was there to help. He remained one of the former president's closest associates, defending Nixon to the end. Rebozo died in 1998, four years after his famous friend.

# CHAPTER THIRTY-THREE

# Jimmy Carter
## A Southerner Wins the White House

The 1976 election seemed to be a throwback to earlier elections when the Democrats swept the South. Richard Nixon had been forced to resign amid scandal, and his appointed vice president, Gerald Ford, became president. Ford's popularity soared, but he was undone by rising inflation and his pardon of Nixon. The Democrats turned to Jimmy Carter, an almost unknown former Georgia governor. A shift of just 25,000 votes in Ohio and Wisconsin would have given the election to Ford. But Carter's sweep of the South, just four years after the Republicans had swept the region, gave him the winning margin. In Florida, Carter received 1,636,000 votes to 1,469,531 for Ford. A third candidate, Eugene McCarthy, earned 26,643.

Bob Graham, himself a presidential candidate in 2004, campaigned with President Jimmy Carter in Florida. (Photo courtesy of the State Archives of Florida)

Jimmy Carter spends the night in the governor's mansion in Tallahassee during his 1980 reelection campaign. (Photo courtesy of the State Archives of Florida)

## Carter Defeats a Southern Giant

When Jimmy Carter announced his candidacy for president, many people asked the same question: "Jimmy Who?" Working with little money, friends and family members as volunteers, and a pledge of honesty, he scored an upset in the Iowa caucuses over far better-known candidates. His follow-up win in the New Hampshire primary established him as the front-runner.

One by one, more famous candidates dropped out, but one question remained: Could Carter defeat Alabama Governor George Wallace, who had been the dominant political force in the South for a dozen years? Carter represented the New South, while Wallace, a staunch segregationist, represented the Old South.

In 1972 Wallace captured 42 percent of the Florida primary vote, grabbing twice as many votes as his nearest Democratic opponent, Senator Hubert Humphrey. Most people had predicted a Wallace victory in the primary, but what shocked everyone were his margin and the breadth of his victory. He carried every county, including Miami-Dade, which was thought to be a Humphrey stronghold with its liberal, elderly population.

Four years later, it was Carter who handed Wallace a defeat, although he did it with just 34 percent of the vote. Wallace received 30 percent, and Senator Henry Jackson got 24 percent. Carter followed his Florida win with a victory in North Carolina, ending Wallace's national ambitions.

# CHAPTER THIRTY-FOUR

# Ronald Reagan
## A Speech that Made History

The presidency of Jimmy Carter was plagued by problems. Rampant inflation, the capture of Americans at the United States embassy in Iran, and Carter's seeming inability to surmount the issues made him vulnerable in 1980. Ronald Reagan, who had lost the 1976 Republican nomination to Gerald Ford, emerged as the Republican nominee. Reagan won in a landslide, winning by more than eight million votes and swamping Carter in the Electoral College: 489 to 49. Florida voters, who went for Carter by more than 150,000 votes in 1976, went for Reagan by a 600,000-vote margin. Republican-turned-independent John Anderson received 189,692 votes, and Libertarian Edward Clark got 30,524. In 1984 Reagan did even better. He received more than ten million more popular votes than in 1980 and carried every state except Massachusetts. In Florida, Reagan received 2,046,951 votes to Democrat Walter Mondale's 1,448,816. Mondale received just thirteen electoral votes. Again, the census had rewarded Florida with more electoral votes, an increase of four to twenty-one.

## The Speech that Almost Never Was

It has become one of the most famous presidential speeches ever given, and two words from the speech have become almost a cliché, used to describe a host of things. Today it is known simply as the "evil empire" speech, and many credit it with launching a campaign that would eventually help topple Communism. But the speech was almost never delivered.

In 1982, when Ronald Reagan spoke to the British Parliament, early drafts of his speech labeled Soviet Russia as the "focus of evil." American diplomats urged caution, and the speech was toned down, but Reagan's desire to make a highly critical speech was not lessened.

Nine months later, Reagan was scheduled to speak to the National Association of Evangelicals at a hotel in Orlando. At the White House, Reagan speechwriters prepared a foreign policy speech that used the words "evil empire." His aides fretted that it was too strong, but Reagan wanted the phrase included. Over the objections of aides, the phrase stayed in.

On March 8, 1983, Reagan flew to Orlando. His first stop was at Disney World's Epcot Center. Reagan had a rich history with Walt Disney and the Disney organization, having been one of the original hosts when Disneyland first opened in California in 1955. At Epcot, Reagan watched a film highlighting American history, met with foreign exchange students, and then spoke to math and science students. In the afternoon, he left Disney World for the brief trip to the hotel. The twelve hundred delegates of the National Association of Evangelicals had long been the backbone of Reagan's support and had suggested that Reagan speak on the subject of

Ronald Reagan's 1985 inauguration was held with the temperature near zero. The outdoor activities were can-celed. In May some of the bands unable to perform on Inauguration Day played for President and Mrs. Reagan at EPCOT. (Photo courtesy of Corbis Images)

religious freedom and the Cold War. They probably assumed they would hear a speech about faith and religion. What they heard instead was a major foreign policy speech. Reagan's speech was 17 pages long, and his reference to the "evil empire" did not come until page 15: "So in your discussions of the nuclear freeze proposals I urge you to beware the temptation of pride—the temptation to blithely declare yourselves above it all and label both sides equally at fault, to ignore the facts of history and the aggressive impulses of an evil empire. . . . "

Anthony Lewis, a columnist for *The New York Times*, called the speech "primitive" and "dangerous," and Senator Edward M. Kennedy said he thought Reagan was more interested in preparing for a nuclear war than preventing one. Nearly a decade later, Reagan spoke to the 1992 Republican National Convention and recalled the Orlando speech: "We stood tall and proclaimed that communism was destined for the ash heap of history. We never heard so much ridicule from our liberal friends. The only thing that got them more upset was two simple words: 'evil empire.' "

# CHAPTER THIRTY-FIVE

# George H.W. Bush
## A Lifelong Lover of Florida

By 1988 Florida had become a fairly predictable Republican state. Republicans won eight of the ten presidential elections from 1952 to 1984. George H.W. Bush easily won in 1988, defeating Michael Dukakis by seven million votes nationally and a million votes in Florida.

## From Fighting to Fishing, a President Turns to Florida

Presidents have fished in Florida for more than 130 years. Grover Cleveland and Chester Arthur found great fishing, and Herbert Hoover once held a state record. But the title of First Fisherman goes to George H.W. Bush, who has been visiting Florida since he was a child. During World War II, he was commissioned an ensign in Corpus Christi, and in June 1943, he was sent to Fort Lauderdale to train on the TBF Avenger torpedo bomber. He stayed there for three months before shipping out to the Pacific.

President George Bush and his grandson prepare for another day of fishing in the Florida Keys. (Photo courtesy of Cheeca Lodge)

He became a frequent visitor after the war, known for his deepwater fishing skills. When Bush began visiting the island of Islamorada to fish and relax, the owners of the Cheeca Lodge wanted to start a fishing tournament called the Presidential. In 1994 Bush became involved, and the tournament began raising money for charity. Now called

President Bush talks to fishermen at his tournament in the Florida Keys. (Photo courtesy of Cheeca Lodge)

the George Bush Cheeca Lodge Bonefish Tournament, it's an official event on the World Billfish Series tour, which determines the world champion angler.

Although thought of as a Texas family, the Bush family has strong ties to Florida. George H. W. Bush's parents owned a home in Hobe Sound; his son, George W. Bush, was active in a Florida campaign in 1968; and his son, Jeb, served two terms as governor.

The Cheeca Lodge in the Florida Keys is home to a fishing tournament sponsored by former President George H.W. Bush. (Photo courtesy of the State Archives of Florida)

# CHAPTER THIRTY-SIX

# George W. Bush
## A President Who Started in Florida

In the 2000 election, Democratic Vice President Al Gore won the popular vote, but lost the election. Gore received 51,003,926 votes to 50,460,110 votes for Texas Governor George W. Bush.

In the 2004 election, Bush had an easier time in the popular vote, but the electoral vote was very close. A shift of 60,000 votes in Ohio would have given the election to John Kerry. In Florida, Bush received 3,964,522 votes to Kerry's 3,583,544 and Nader's 32,971. Nader, who had played such a huge role in 2000, was little more than a footnote in 2004. The state's electoral vote count increased again as a result of the 2000 census, bringing the total to twenty-seven.

President George Bush came to Florida early in his administration to announce his support for the Everglades National Park. To his left is his brother, Governor Jeb Bush. (Photo courtesy of the State Archives of Florida)

## The First Campaign of George W. Bush

George W. Bush will forever be linked to Florida because of the dispute over the 2000 presidential election, but Bush participated in an earlier election in Florida that was actually nastier than the one in 2000. In 1968 Bush graduated from Yale University and, like many young men that year, knew he faced the draft. Rather than be forced into military service, he joined the Texas Air National Guard but didn't begin flight training until November at Moody Air Force Base in Georgia. In the interim, Bush was introduced to the tough world of Florida politics.

For Florida politics, 1968 was an unusual year. The Republicans were newly resurgent, having captured the governor's mansion two years earlier for the first time in nearly a century. Alabama Governor George Wallace was running for president as an Independent and making civil rights a major issue in Florida and across the nation. The 1968 Florida Senate race was a nasty affair. Bush moved to Orlando to work for Edward Gurney, a congressman from nearby Winter Park. Gurney was running his first statewide campaign after three terms in the House. His opponent was Leroy Collins Jr., widely credited with being Florida's greatest governor and the man selected as Florida's most outstanding politician in the twentieth century. During the 1950s, he served six years as the state's governor, earning a reputation for honest leadership and a moderate record on civil rights.

Collins left office with the admiration of most Floridians and in 1965 accepted a position as director of the Community Relations Service from President Lyndon Johnson. The job had been created by the 1964 Civil Rights Act, and one of his duties was to act as a go-between for civil rights demonstrators and local officials. The job took him to Selma, Alabama, site of one of the major demonstrations of the civil rights movement. During the march, a photograph was taken of Collins with Dr. Martin Luther King Jr. It looked as though the former Florida governor was one of the leaders of the march.

One of the assignments Bush was given was to mail the Selma photograph to newspapers and leaders in Florida. The picture went out without any caption, leaving it to the recipients to figure out what the image meant. They usually drew the same conclusion: that Collins was a supporter of Dr. King and the marchers. The photograph of King and Collins is generally credited with helping Gurney win an easy victory in the Senate race. In 1974, however, Gurney was indicted in an influence-peddling scandal and didn't seek reelection. A political comeback attempt failed, and he died largely forgotten, while Floridians' respect for Collins continued to increase.

Bush had another job in the 1968 campaign, which he called the "pillow job." Gurney had been wounded during World War II, and it was extremely painful for him to sit down. He carried a pillow with him at all times, which made it difficult during the campaign to shake hands with constituents. In addition, the pillow was a distraction. Bush's job was to tote the pillow and hand it to Gurney when he sat down.

## Florida Again Decides a Presidential Election

On election night in 2000, Vice President Al Gore called Texas Governor George Bush to concede the race. Gore believed he had lost a close election, but as the nation soon learned, the matter was far from settled. When the polls closed in Florida at 8 P.M., the television networks declared that Gore had won the key state of Florida. The rest of the nation was less encouraging for Gore, and at 2:15 A.M. the next day, the major networks called the election for Bush, proclaiming him the new president-elect. What's more, Florida had swung the other way, prompting predictions that Gore lost the state by about fifty thousand votes.

But as Gore was on his way to give his concession speech in Nashville, aides reached him and said the election was in doubt. Two hours after proclaiming Bush the winner, the networks reported that the election was undecided and the Florida results were fluid, now shifting back toward Gore. By morning, questions began to arise about irregular voting, particularly in Palm Beach County. Both campaigns sent attorneys to Florida to look out for their clients' interests. Bush's team was the first to go to court to try to stop the recounts. The Democrats responded with their own suits. Republican Secretary of State Katherine Harris, under Governor Jeb Bush, brother of George W. Bush, did her best to stop the recounts as the Bush lead shrunk to just 286 votes.

On November 21, the Florida Supreme Court ruled that recounts could continue and gave the counties five days to finish up. But Bush took his case to the United States Supreme Court, asking that the recount be stopped. To the surprise of many, the high court agreed to hear the case.

Harris certified the state results and gave Bush a 537-vote lead. But Harris didn't include final results from heavily Democratic Palm Beach County. On December 9, the United States Supreme Court ordered the recounts stopped and scheduled a hearing for December 11. At that hearing, Bush's attorneys argued that the Florida Supreme Court had overstepped the boundaries of its powers by ordering the recounts. Gore's attorneys argued that the U.S. Supreme Court had no reason to intervene. The following day, the Supreme Court ruled in favor of Bush, and the election was over.

Bush lost the national popular vote—50,999,897 to 50,456,002— but won the White House because of his majority in the Electoral College. In crucial Florida, Bush's final, official total was 2,912,790 votes to Gore's 2,912,253. Green Party candidate Ralph Nader received 97,488 votes; Pat Buchanan, 17,484; and Libertarian Harry Browne, 16,415.

## Could It Have Been a Different President Bush?

The question is impossible to answer, but it is fascinating to wonder which son was the logical political heir of former President George H.W. Bush. Of course, it was George W. Bush who went on to the White House, but there are those who believe that Jeb, not George, was the Bush who should have inherited the family mantle.

Both George and Jeb ran for governorships in 1994, their first tries at winning political office. Both ran against incumbents: George Bush against Ann Richards in Texas, and Jeb Bush against Lawton Chiles in Florida. Many thought Jeb Bush had a better chance of winning than his brother. Richards had a commanding lead, while Chiles was considered much more vulnerable. Some people thought George Bush was running against Richards only to get revenge for the nasty, mocking things she had said about his father at the 1988 Democratic National Convention: "Poor

George—he can't help it. He was born with a silver foot in his mouth."

The brothers had the advantage of running in what turned out to be a Republican year. The administration of Democrat Bill Clinton had stumbled during its first two years, primarily by alienating Americans over a botched health care plan. Across the country, Democrats were in trouble.

Richards failed to take her opponent seriously, dismissing him as "some jerk." George W. Bush defeated Richards by a 53% to 47% percent margin. In Florida, Chiles did take Jeb Bush seriously and ran a tough campaign. He held on by a single percentage point. Jeb Bush had lost despite a Republican landslide. The Democratic governor lost not only in Texas but also in New York. The Republicans took control of Congress.

Jeb Bush returned four years later and won the Florida governorship, but by then his brother George had four years of national attention behind him and was already being mentioned as a possible presidential contender. In 2007 journalist and author Shirish Date wrote an article for *The Washington Post* speculating on what might have been. He imagined it was Jeb, not George, who had been elected in 2000. He thought Jeb, "the articulate and handsome workaholic," would have made a better president, pointing out that Jeb is much more detail-oriented and likes to govern.

Jeb Bush may yet be a candidate for president—his older brother thought he should have run in 2012—but the question will always linger: What if?

## The President Learns of a Terrorist Attack

No one will ever forget where he or she was on September 11, 2001, as the towers of the World Trade Center collapsed and an airplane smashed into the Pentagon. George W. Bush will certainly remember where he was. It is difficult to imagine a more unusual juxtaposition: images of the terror attacks alongside images of Bush, sitting in an elementary school in Sarasota, listening to second graders read *The Pet Goat.*

As he entered the school, he was told that a plane had crashed into the World Trade Center, but the details were sketchy and he thought it was an accident, a pilot in a light plane had struck the building

As he listened to the students read, Bush's chief of staff, Andrew Card, approached and whispered news of the second attack. The expression on Bush's face told the students that something was seriously wrong, yet he stayed for another few minutes. Critics later complained that Bush lingered too long while America was under attack, but most praised him for not showing signs of panic. Principal Gwendolyn Tose-Rigell later said, "I don't think anyone could have handled it better. What would it have served if [Bush] had jumped out of his chair and run out of the room?"

Different stories have emerged about what happened in Sarasota that morning. But retired Sarasota School Superintendent Wilma Hamilton clearly remembers that as she waited to enter the classroom with Bush, he was told a plane had struck the World Trade Center. He told her that he might not be able to stay as long as scheduled. But in describing the incident to Hamilton, Bush called what had happened an "accident."

When he left the classroom, he went to another room to meet with aides. He emerged a short time later and went to the school media center to talk with reporters. At 9:30 a.m., Bush said there had been "an apparent terrorist attack." He announced that he was returning to Washington, but the Secret Service considered the situation there unstable. The president left for the Sarasota-Bradenton International Airport and flew not to Washington, but to Barksdale Air Force Base in Louisiana, then to Offutt Air Force Base in Nebraska, and finally back to the capitol.

# CHAPTER THIRTY-SEVEN

# Barack Obama
## An Oil Spill Threatens Florida and Obama

Republican presidential candidate John McCain carried most of the South in the 2008 election, in most cases with double-digit victories. But Florida moved back to the Democratic Party, choosing Illinois Senator Barack Obama by a comfortable margin. Nationally, Obama won by nearly 10 million popular votes and 192 electoral votes. In Florida, Obama outpolled McCain by more than 200,000 votes: 4,282,074 to 4,045,624.

### Come On In, The Water's Fine

On April 20, 2010, the BP oil spill in the Gulf of Mexico threatened Florida's tourism and fishing industries and handed President Barack Obama a major challenge to his presidency.

Before it was capped in mid-July, nearly five million barrels of oil had spilled into the gulf and there was extensive damage to marine and wildlife habitats. Although Louisiana sustained most of the damage, the coast around Pensacola was threatened.

Almost immediately vacationers began canceling their plans to visit Florida's Panhandle, and there was early speculation that the oil could spread along Florida's west coast and then up the east coast. Throughout the nation, television viewers saw dead fish and birds on the Florida Panhandle beaches, and reporters held globs of oil to show the threat.

Restaurants refused to buy fish from the gulf, and soon thousands of fishermen were out of work.

While it was a crisis for Florida, it was also a crisis for Obama. At first, the Administration let British Petroleum take the lead in capping the well, containing the oil spill, and cleaning up the mess.

Obama was criticized for not paying enough attention to the spill. He defended his administration saying, "I'm confident people are going to look back and say this administration was on top of what was an unprecedented crisis."

As the criticism on Obama mounted, the president staged a series of media events to show he was involved. He sent a string of administration officials to Florida to monitor the situation.

Obama made four trips to the gulf coast to show his commitment, and Mrs. Obama came twice. Finally, in mid August, the Obama family came to Panama City for a weekend vacation. He wanted to show Americans that the beach was clean and ready for tourists.

There was one question about the Obama vacation that captivated the media—would he be photographed without his shirt on? Shortly after his election in 2008, the President was photographed swimming in Hawaii and looking very fit.

White House reporters wondered not only if Obama would go swimming, but if he would put his well-toned pecs on display.

Obama did go in the gulf water with his daughter Sasha and showed that it was safe to swim. But White House photographers were kept at bay, and the only photo taken didn't show Obama's chest, just his head sticking out of the water.

President Obama and his daughter Sasha swam in the Gulf of Mexico to show it was safe following the giant oil spill. (Photo courtesy of Corbis Images)

Barack Obama speaks at Disney World in 2012 with Cinderella's castle as a backdrop. (Photo courtesy of Corbis Images)

# CHAPTER THIRTY-EIGHT

# *Presidents at Resorts*
## *Florida Resorts Prove to Be a Major Attraction*

For more than a century, Florida's resorts have attracted presidents as well as tourists. Where the presidents went—and where they stayed—has reflected the state's changing tourism patterns.

If there is one resort that functions as a second home to presidents, it's the sprawling Fontainebleau Hotel in Miami Beach. The hotel opened in 1954 on the site of what had been the estate of tire magnate Harvey Firestone and has hosted every president since Dwight Eisenhower.

The Breakers in Palm Beach has been the state's grandest resort for nearly a century. The original hotel, built by Henry Flagler, burned down

Lyndon Johnson shakes hands outside the Fontainebleau Hotel in Miami. (Photo courtesy of the State Archives of Florida)

and was replaced by an even grander structure. Presidents Gerald Ford, Ronald Reagan, George H.W. Bush, and Bill Clinton have stayed in the seventeen-hundred-square-foot Imperial Suite, which features handmade carpets, marble floors, and hand-carved ceilings.

The Don Cesar Hotel was built just as the Florida land boom of the 1920s was coming to a disastrous end. Located on St. Petersburg Beach, the hotel was a favorite of some of the biggest names of the era, such as F. Scott Fitzgerald, Clarence Darrow, and Al Capone. It has also played host to Franklin Roosevelt, Gerald Ford, Jimmy Carter, Bill Clinton, and George W. Bush. The giant pink structure was taken over by the government during World War II, was nearly ruined by government renovations, and then was abandoned for years. It has since been restored to its 1920s' grandeur.

The Biltmore in Coral Gables was another product of the Florida land boom, built at a cost of $10 million. Like the Don Cesar, it was a favorite of Al Capone and presidents as well, including Calvin Coolidge, Jimmy Carter, George H.W. Bush, and Bill Clinton.

Hawks Cay Resort in the Florida Keys is not one of the grand resorts, but it is a popular tourist destination. Harry Truman, Dwight

Franklin Roosevelt was the first president to stay at the Don Cesar in St. Petersburg Beach. He took control of the hotel during World War II for military use. (Photo courtesy of the State Archives of Florida)

Eisenhower, and Lyndon Johnson fished and relaxed at the resort on Duck Key. When Truman arrived, a reporter asked him how long he was going to stay. "As long as my money holds out," he replied. Truman started each day with a shot of bourbon and a glass of orange juice, followed by a walk.

Few Florida resorts can claim to have entertained two former presidents at the same time. Harris Rosen, Orlando's largest private hotel owner, hosted former Presidents Clinton and Bush at his Shingle Creek Hotel while the three worked on a project to aid Haiti. (Photo courtesy of Shingle Creek Hotel)

The Vinoy Park Hotel in St. Petersburg opened in 1925 and soon played host to Calvin Coolidge. Oddly enough, the president didn't eat in the grand ballroom, preferring instead to eat in the staff cafeteria. More recently, both former presidents George W. Bush and Bill Clinton were guests of Harris Rosen, owner of the Shingle Creek Hotel. All three were involved in providing disaster relief to residents of Haiti.

With its 1,700-square-foot presidential suite, The Breakers in Palm Beach is a favorite of presidents. (Photo courtesy of the State Archives of Florida)

# CHAPTER THIRTY-NINE

# *Florida in the Primaries*

The Founding Fathers never imagined that there would be a need for political parties, but gradually they evolved. Presidential candidates were selected at national political conventions, which were controlled by political machines. Ordinary voters had little say in determining who the candidates were. In the early 1900s, Florida was going through a progressive era, which led to the creation of the first presidential preference primary in 1904. Although it was nonbinding, the primary gave voters a chance to show how they felt about the candidates. It set off a national trend. The following year, Wisconsin passed legislation creating a primary that selected delegates, and Oregon followed with the first primary that bound delegates to a particular candidate.

Florida may have had the first primary, but it didn't have a truly contested one until 1932, when New York Governor Franklin Roosevelt won 88 percent of the Democratic vote against Governor William Murray of Oklahoma. There wasn't another such contest until 1952, when Georgia Senator Richard Russell defeated Tennessee Senator Estes Kefauver. Kefauver was eventually chosen as the vice presidential candidate. Russell was the leading segregationist in the South, and his support was a show by Southerners that they opposed any civil rights legislation. The Democratic nominee that year was Illinois Governor Adlai Stevenson, who would run again in 1956. That year, he entered the Florida primary and defeated Kefauver by a narrow margin, 52 percent to 48 percent.

Florida had always played a small role in the nominating process. During much of the twentieth century, it had the smallest population in the South. It was a difficult state for candidates to reach in an era before convenient automobile and air travel. Additionally, the Florida primary was always held late, usually after the candidate had been decided.

In 1972 Florida moved its primary to March 14, one of the earliest in the nation. At the same time, Florida was becoming one of the nation's largest states, a prize worth winning. The Democrats had a huge field. Among the eleven candidates were Indiana Senator Vance Hartke, Arkansas Congressman Wilbur Mills, and Los Angeles Mayor Sam Yorty— men well-known at the time but forgotten today. From the start, the contest was for second place. Everyone knew that segregationist Governor George Wallace of Alabama would win the primary but couldn't win the nomination. Senators Hubert Humphrey of Minnesota, Henry Jackson of Washington, George McGovern of South Dakota, and Edmund Muskie of Maine were the favorites to finish second to Wallace. Wallace won easily with 42 percent of the vote. Humphrey could claim a small prize, however. Although he finished with just 19 percent of the vote, he beat Muskie, Jackson, and McGovern. On Florida's Republican ballot, incumbent President Richard Nixon received 87 percent of the primary vote.

In 1976 Florida played a key role in determining the Republican nominee. Ronald Reagan was challenging President Gerald Ford, who had won two key primaries, but Reagan was very strong in the South. A setback for Ford might hand the nomination to Reagan. Ford held on, however, winning with 53 percent of the vote. Without that victory, Ford could have lost the nomination in 1976. Reagan did win the primary in 1980, easily defeating George H.W. Bush by a nearly two-to-one margin.

After 1980 Florida joined the Super Tuesday regional primary and lost its position as a dominant player in Republican politics. Florida voted in 1988 for George H.W. Bush, the eventual Republican nominee and winner in November, but sixteen other states voted the same day, and Florida's impact was largely lost. By abandoning the regional primary, Florida was able to reclaim its national position. In 1996 Bob Dole won the Florida primary with 57 percent of the vote, compared to 20 percent for magazine publisher Steve Forbes and 18 percent for Pat Buchanan.

Florida returned to the national spotlight in 2008 as Republican voters found themselves pulled into a brawl involving Arizona Senator

John McCain and former New York City Mayor Rudy Giuliani. Giuliani tried an unusual strategy: He had skipped the early primaries and bet everything on a win in Florida. But McCain received 36 percent of the vote to Giuliani's 31 percent, ending the New Yorker's campaign. The 2008 Florida primary also made news on the Democratic side, as Hillary Clinton kept her campaign alive with an easy win, 50 percent to 33 percent over Barack Obama.

In 2012 the Republican primary contest was the toughest in history. Candidates and their supporters poured millions of dollars into the state, and candidates traded ever-escalating charges. In the end, former Massachusetts Governor Mitt Romney easily won the primary.

# Bibliographic Essay

More than one hundred sources were used in the preparation of this book, ranging from standard textbooks, books of popular history, historical journals, newspaper articles, research libraries, and recognized Internet sites.

The two standard texts of Florida history remain *The New History of Florida,* edited by Michael Gannon (University Press of Florida, 1996), and *A History of Florida* by Charlton W. Tebeau and William Marina (University of Miami Press, 1999).

For historians seeking to do research on the presidency, the best starting place is the Miller Center at the University of Virginia. The nonpartisan center (millercenter.org) has created a wealth of information and sources for any scholar. For research in Florida history, the starting place remains the P.K. Yonge Library at the University of Florida. The library has a wealth of maps and documents about Florida. The American Presidency Project at the University of California Santa Barbara (presidency.ucsb.edu) has presidential speeches, papers, and transcripts of press conferences. The project contains more than 100,000 presidential documents, including the press conferences of Dwight Eisenhower and Richard Nixon, which are used in this book.

The state of Florida has established websites with valuable information for someone willing to navigate confusing sites. A good starting place is flheritage.com. Most valuable is the detailed bibliography maintained by the Florida Department of State at dlis.dos.state.fl.us/library/bibliographies.

Many of the articles in this book relied on the *Florida Historical Quarterly.* The quarterly is available through JSTOR (jstor.org). Articles that I relied on include "East Florida in the American Revolution, 1775–1778," "Florida's Live Oak Farm of John Quincy Adams," "Florida Fails a Presidential Bid," "Claude Pepper, Strom Thurmond, and the 1948 Presidential Election in Florida," "Grant Forecasts the Future of Florida," "Florida and the Presidential Election of 1928," and "Zangara's Attempted

Assassination of Franklin D. Roosevelt."

James W. Covington's *The Seminoles of Florida* (University Press of Florida, 1993), remains the best source for the coverage of the Seminole Indian Wars.

The four-hundred-year-long battle over a proposed Cross-Florida Barge Canal is best described in *Ditch of Dreams* by Steven Noll and David Tegeder (University Press of Florida, 2009). *The Door of Hope: Republican Presidents and the First Southern Strategy,* 1877–1933 (University Press of Florida, 2011) contains valuable information about Republican presidents in Florida.

Florida writer Ray Osborne has done groundbreaking research into the Florida visits by Warren G. Harding, Franklin D. Roosevelt, and Grover Cleveland. He is also a leading writer about Cape Canaveral and Cocoa Beach. He can be contacted at *ourhistory153@yahoo.com.*

Newspapers played a major role in assembling information about this book. *The New York Times* covered presidential trips to the South, as did *Harper's Weekly.* In Florida, a number of newspapers were utilized, including *The Florida Times-Union, St. Petersburg Times, Miami Herald, Tampa Tribune, Tallahassee Democrat,* and *Orlando Sentinel.*

Two men have probably done the most to save and spread the wonderful stories that make up Florida history. In this book, I utilized two of the books in the *Florida Chronicles* series of the late Stuart B. McIver: *Dreamers, Schemers and Scalawags* (Pineapple Press, 1994) and *Touched by the Sun* (Pineapple Press, 2001). In the 1970s, *Florida Trend,* the state's leading business publication, began publishing monthly history columns by the late Gene Burnett. They seemed out of place in a business publication, but the readers loved them. They were assembled in a series of three volumes entitled *Florida's Past: People and Events That Have Shaped the State,* and have been reissued in paperback (Pineapple Press, 1996, 1997).

The photographs in this book come primarily from the Florida Department of State's Florida Memory project (floridamemory.com), a treasure chest of thousands of pictures and maps.

# Index

*Bold page numbers indicate illustrations*

Here are some other books from Pineapple Press on related topics. For a complete catalog, write to Pineapple Press, P.O. Box 3889, Sarasota, Florida 34230-3889, or call (800) 746-3275. Or visit our website at www.pineapplepress.com.

*200 Quick Looks at Florida History* by James C. Clark. Packed with unusual and little-known facts and stories about the Sunshine State. For example, the inventor of air conditioning died broke and forgotten; Florida printed $3 bills in the 1830s; and Florida's first tourist attraction featured ostrich racing. A crash course in Florida history!

*The Florida Chronicles* by Stuart B. McIver. A series offering true-life sagas of the notable and notorious characters throughout history who have given Florida its distinctive flavor. **Volume 1**: *Dreamers, Schemers and Scalawags*; **Volume 2**: *Murder in the Tropics*; **Volume 3**: *Touched by the Sun*

*Florida's Past* Volumes 1, 2, and 3 by Gene Burnett. Collected essays from Burnett's "Florida's Past" columns in *Florida Trend* magazine, plus some original writings not found elsewhere. Burnett's easygoing style and his sometimes surprising choice of topics make history good reading.

*Discovering the Civil War in Florida,* Second Edition, by Paul Taylor. This important book for Civil War and Florida history buffs has been updated with even more official government reports and firsthand reports by soldiers on both sides of the conflict. Several sites have also been added to the guide for visiting Civil War sites.

*Time Traveler's Guide to Florida* by Jack Powell. This unique guidebook offers 140 places in Florida where you can experience the past, as well as a few where you can time-travel into the future! You can join in all kinds of historical reenactments—in full costume, if you like.

*Historical Traveler's Guide to Florida,* Second Edition, by Eliot Kleinberg. From Fort Pickens in the Panhandle to Fort Jefferson in the ocean forty miles beyond Key West, historical travelers will find many adventures waiting for them in Florida. The author presents seventy-four of his favorites, seventeen of which are new to this edition. The rest have been completely updated.

*The Edisons of Fort Myers* by Tom Smoot. Discover the fascinating story of Thomas and Mina Edison during the forty-six years they wintered in Fort Myers. Visit the extensive botanical gardens Thomas created and tended, as well as his famous laboratory. Learn about his friendship with carmaker Henry Ford and tire magnate Harvey Firestone.